A Jew in the Woods

PAGES FROM A DIARY

A Jew in the Woods

PAGES FROM A DIARY

by

Berl Kagan

TRANSLATED BY
MAX ROSENFELD

A Jew in the Woods: Pages from a Diary
By Berl Kagan
Translated by Max Rosenfeld
Introduction by Rebecca Frankel

White Goat Press, the Yiddish Book Center's imprint
Yiddish Book Center
Amherst, MA 01002
whitegoatpress.org

Printed in the United States of America at The Studley Press, Dalton, MA
10 9 8 7 6 5 4 3 2 1

Paperback ISBN 979-8-9987798-6-2
Ebook ISBN 979-8-9987798-7-9

Library of Congress Control Number: 2026933778

Book design by Michael Grinley
Cover design by Kandy Littrell

Pictured on the front cover is Berl Kagan's original handwritten diary, donated upon his death in 1993 by his daughter, Miriam Kagan Lieber, to the Archives of the YIVO Institute for Jewish Research in New York.

Front cover photograph:
From the Archives of the YIVO Institute for Jewish Research, New York.

The publication of this book is made possible with generous support from Muriel and Laurence Gillick.

Sanctified is the memory of
the most succulent branch cut down from our
nation's tree—the Jews of Eastern Europe.

—Berl Kagan

Introduction

BY REBECCA FRANKEL

On March 28, 1944, exiled Dutch education minister Gerrit Bolkestein made an appeal to his fellow countrymen. During a BBC radio broadcast from London, Bolkestein asked listeners still under German occupation in the Netherlands to participate in an unexpected campaign of resistance. The mighty weapon of choice? A pen.

"History cannot be written on the basis of official decisions and documents alone," Bolkestein argued, and he implored listeners to put their experiences on paper in "a diary or letters." By his reasoning, only through the simple, daily accounts of ordinary citizens could official records be contextualized and the country's "struggle for freedom be painted in full depth and shine."

Under any other circumstances, Bolkestein's mission would have seemed entirely mundane, but during war the act would prove essential, even dangerous. The Dutch people were inspired. At the end of the war, the National Office for the History of the Netherlands in Wartime collected more than two thousand volumes.

Among those listening to Bolkestein on March 28 was a 14-year-old Jewish girl in Amsterdam who was already writing what is arguably the most famous diary of all time—*The Diary of a Young Girl*. Or, as the posthumous publication of her writings is more commonly known, *The Diary of Anne Frank*.

If Bolkestein's BBC broadcast made news across Europe, it's doubtful word of it reached Berl Kagan, the author of this diary, who was, at the time, some 1,300 miles away, in Karalgiris, Lithuania. But like young Anne Frank, Kagan was already at work preserving his account of the war that was likewise destined for publication. Kagan was also fully aware of the risk he—an escaped Jew in hiding from the Nazis—was taking to write it.

As Kagan explains in the book's introduction, at first he "kept the diary in a disguised form," camouflaging names, dates, and locations in the hopes it would "lessen our peril should the notes fall into the hands of the Germans." Kagan quickly abandoned the disguise once he realized it did little more than foster a "naive delusion" of safety. By his own calculations, his chances of surviving were already near zero.

For ten long, harrowing months, Kagan kept regular journal entries on the only paper he could find—two small, used copy books left behind in a butcher shop. In between the already filled-in lines of those notepads, Kagan vividly recorded the time that he, his wife, Raja, and sister-in-law, Nechama (and occasionally a handful of other escaped Jewish refugees), spent in hiding. Their group found fragile sanctuary on a rural farm belonging to two Lithuanian peasants, Tadeusz and Barbora, and in the dense forest area surrounding the elderly couple's home.

From the journal's first entry, dated Oct. 20, 1943, Kagan conveyed all manner of their struggle to survive, beginning with the aftermath of their daring escape from the Kovno Ghetto. He described the stark existence of hiding both in a barn's haystack and the raw, inhospitable forest, where in the winter they battled the slush, snow, and frigid temperatures and in the summer warded off fleas, lice, ticks, and often-fatal diseases. Within weeks of arriving in Karalgiris, Kagan wrote, "We have exchanged our life in a city filled with people for a dog and a forest. We have traveled from the 20th century back to the Dark Ages."

He wrote of the dizzying number of miles they trekked in and out of the woods to avoid discovery, running back and forth to their rescuers' single-room farmhouse. Their precarious circumstances included numerous near-captures that crippled them with fear. "The sound is moving in our direction. Our limbs feel paralyzed. Is one of those men coming to search the bushes? It's too late now for us to run. We press our faces to the ground and hover between life and death."

There was always the chance Kagan's family would run out of

food or that one of their rescuers would have a change of heart and turn them in to local police. In his final journal entry, from August 1944, Kagan shared the fleeting joy of their liberation and the sad return to Kovno, their devastated hometown.

The result of all Kagan's painstaking record-keeping is this remarkable book, *A Jew in the Woods: Pages from a Diary*. It is a rare, if not singular, Holocaust-era artifact.

It might seem counterintuitive, even odd, to say that a book originally published in 1955 stands to shed new light on the Holocaust experience, seventy years later. Especially as *A Jew in the Woods* received significant attention upon its original Yiddish publication from one of Jewish literature's most lauded writers, Isaac Bashevis Singer, who reviewed it for *The Forward*, one of the most widely read Jewish newspapers of the time.

But this translation of *A Jew in the Woods* brings with it the opportunity to rediscover this history through the most intimate of lenses. It offers the chance to enrich a little-explored topic of World War II history, one that is often left out of the broader canon of Holocaust narratives: the Jews who escaped Nazi persecution and fled to the woods of Eastern Europe.

There does not exist, in any collected form, a universal, authoritative history detailing the Jewish experience in the woods during the Holocaust. Nor is there a central archive of documentation coordinated around the forest experience with a database of names of victims or survivors who went into the woods to hide before or after they were interned into ghettos by the Nazis. There are no official tallies. The numbers historians rely on are estimates based on known survivors. I first encountered this dearth of history and the lack of understanding around it while writing *Into the Forest: A Holocaust Story of Survival, Triumph, and Love*, a nonfiction account of a Polish Jewish family, the Rabinowitzes, who, like the Kagans, escaped their ghetto. They fled to the nearby forest, where they survived in a family camp for two years.

I was able to write *Into the Forest* primarily by interviewing the Rabinowitz family's two daughters and a few survivors who were with them in the woods. During the more than five years I spent researching and reporting, I deployed all the journalistic skills I had in order to give context and add detail to these women's childhood experiences and their decades-old memories. I consulted historians and academics. I listened to testimonies of other Holocaust survivors who fled to the woods of Eastern Europe. I read memoirs of Jewish partisans and many Yizkor memorial books. I watched dozens of hours of survivor interviews. I plumbed the depths of municipal records from various countries. I even scoured decades-old genealogy message boards, examining everything and anything I could find that might help me understand what it was like for this family to survive in the woods for two whole years.

It was not easy. All these resources were rich and valuable, but connecting all they had to offer into a larger narrative was like putting together a puzzle with many pieces scattered or hidden from view. I found myself daydreaming of time travel or wishing to unearth some long-forgotten notebook exactly like Berl Kagan's diary. But in the woods, where men made makeshift playing cards out of tree bark, it seemed impossible that something like a journal could have existed.

This deficit of forest history and its long and frequent omission from the broader canon of Holocaust history can be explained by a number of factors.

Firstly, we look to the record. Unlike the Nazis' meticulous cataloging of their ghettos, concentration camps, and mobile death squads, there are few authoritative (or institutional) documents pertaining to the population of Jews who ran to the forest. The Soviets certainly kept records of their partisan networks, which included Jewish fighters, but for decades they suppressed the narrative of Jewish partisan activity. The *Einsatzgruppen* (German death squad) memos mention Jewish refugees in the woods, but only those who were taken prisoner or killed.

Historian Yitzhak Arad addressed this in his paper "Jewish Family Camps in the Forest—an Original Means of Rescue," which he presented at the Yad Vashem International Historical Conference in April 1974. Arad wrote, "There are no exact statistics on the number of Jews who were saved in this manner, nor is it known how many Jews found refuge in the family camps." He determined therefore that the number of these Jews who availed themselves of the forest, for better or worse, could never be known. Arad leaves us to conclude that there will never be accurate numbers because no such lists exist.

The few published works on the subject are largely memoirs (many now out of print) and piecemeal analyses found in anthologies; the most famous is a Jewish partisan narrative about the Bielski brothers, whose story has been told in multiple books. (Nechama Tec's book about the brothers, *Defiance*, was adapted into a 2008 film starring actors Daniel Craig and Liev Schreiber.)

Further explaining this lack of attention likely has much to do with the fact that those who took shelter in the forest represent a very small population of the Jews who endured the Holocaust.

Historians estimate that 25,000 Jewish refugees escaped to the woods of Eastern Europe. Of these, more than 15,000 Jewish men and women joined the Soviet partisans to fight against the Germans. In his 1974 paper, Arad calculated that 10,000 others lived in small, splintered family camps or, like Berl, Raja, and Nechama, survived in hiding with the help of non-Jews.

Arad also noted that "The number of Jews who reached the forests was much larger than the number who were alive when the Soviet Army liberated the area in the summer of 1944." And though we may never be able to know the forest population precisely, we can be sure it was a mere fraction of the millions of people who suffered in the Nazi concentration camps.

For perspective, consider the Kovno Ghetto survivors. When the Nazis sealed the ghetto there in 1941, there were 35,000 Jews interned in its boundaries. Of that number, it's believed that only five hundred Jews managed to escape the ghetto and survive in the woods. Berl, Raja, and Nechama were among this very small group.

If we want to learn more about the Jews of the forest or the Righteous Gentiles who saved them, our only recourse is to turn to personal accounts—interviews, testimony, memoirs, and now a diary.

•●•●

In his 1979 introduction to the book *Jewish Responses to Nazi Persecution* (which includes more than sixty eyewitness testimonies of Jewish survivors), esteemed archivist and historian Isaiah Trunk defended the importance of first-hand accounts and their standing in Holocaust archives. "Eyewitness documents of the Holocaust are particularly valuable in bringing to light a wide range of Holocaust phenomena for which they are the major, and frequently the *only*, authentic source."

With *A Jew in the Woods*, Berl Kagan the diarist and documentarian proved—and now proves again—Trunk's point. In a wise decision Kagan chose not to rewrite his diary for publication, and he edited the passages only sparingly. As Kagan explained in his 1955 introduction, most of the diary's entries were recorded "as the events happened or immediately afterward so that as much as possible of the hot breath of the actual experience would remain."

This is the critical distinction between capturing moments in real time and tracking accounts in official catalogs. It's why this diary has the power to bring the forest life experience to the fore on an entirely new and more intimate level. It reinforces why having a window into the daily life in the woods is noteworthy.

Isaac Bashevis Singer may not have been able to fully appreciate this when he wrote his review of *A yid in vald* in 1956. "[Kagan's] diary is a seldom-recorded document," Singer wrote in *The Forward*. "It should be translated in all languages." Brief words of praise, yes, and in my view a wholly inadequate appreciation.

It's likely that Singer's limited perspective was a result of timing. Where I was able to immerse myself in a long review of this history and mountains of archival materials (disparate though they were), World War II was barely ten years in the world's rearview mirror when Kagan's diary was originally published.

But in a single line Singer beautifully surmised what made Berl Kagan a special writer and a worthy keeper of the history he illuminates in his diary. "*A Jew in the Woods* is a tiny book, but the whole Jewish and human tragedy is there in these pages."

Kagan had a keen gift for clear-eyed observation, reconstructing dialogue, and crafting lyric prose. He is an equitable narrator who didn't shy away from self-criticism. More important, Kagan relayed not just his family's circumstances but also the emotional stakes of what they survived. With great compassion and humanity, Kagan presents a full portrait of the refugees' relationship with their rescuers, Tadeusz and Barbora. Even when the trust between them was at its most tenuous, Kagan remained fully cognizant of what the Lithuanian farmers were risking to save the lives of his group.

Despite the grueling hardships and all their reasons for despair, Kagan was capable of marveling at the birds and expressing gratitude for the warmth of the sun. Nor did he abandon his deep reverence for the sanctity of hope. Six months into their hiding he wrote, "In the ghetto and in the barn I learned to keep quiet while someone else was saying things that expressed hope and faith in deliverance, even though I didn't believe it. To express doubts, except in a moment of real danger, means to commit spiritual theft."

It's hard to imagine that when Gerrit Bolkestein gave his 1944 broadcast in the hope of securing his country's history for future generations, the exiled Dutch minister could have foreseen what would follow after the war. Or that he could have imagined the tremendous impact ordinary citizens and their accounts would have on the collective record of World War II. But his instincts were prescient, even profound. Certainly, the "full depth and shine" of Holocaust history came from individuals. Anne Frank's influence on the world's understanding of the Holocaust, after all, is undeniable. Since its original publication in 1947, *The Diary of a Young Girl* has been translated into seventy languages and sold more than thirty million copies around the globe.

I don't think it's an exaggeration to say that for the Jews who fled to the forest, Berl Kagan's diary brings fuller depth and shine to their history. It is only now, seventy years later, that we can fully appreciate it.

—*Rebecca Frankel*

Rebecca Frankel is the author of *Into the Forest: A Holocaust Story of Survival, Triumph, and Love,* a 2021 National Jewish Book Award finalist.

Prologue

BY BERL KAGAN

In the second half of 1943 the Jews in the Slabodka Ghetto lost any remaining illusions they still might have had that they would survive Hitler's reign. The news that reached us concerning the mass liquidation of 99 percent of the ghettos, the hints by Nazi leaders that they intended to destroy all the Jews, the little faith we had that the Soviet military advance would pick up sufficient momentum to prevent the Germans from liquidating the last few ghettos—all these considerations sharply reduced the number of optimists inside the Slabodka Ghetto. The conviction became more and more widespread that if any escape were possible at all, it was only through the barbed wire fence. Jewish organizations, political parties, and individuals feverishly began making plans. But escape to where? There were only two possibilities: the forest or the countryside. The former meant joining the partisans; the latter meant finding a peasant who would provide a hiding place.

The organizations were thinking mainly about the former alternative; individuals about the latter.

The problem with joining the partisans was much more complex in the Slabodka Ghetto than it was in other ghettos. Even at that late date there was no partisan movement in the area around Kaunas (Kovno), and to the extent that one was in the early stages of formation, there was no contact yet between it and the newly forming Jewish partisan cells inside the ghetto. Partisan activity at that time existed only in areas that were a great distance from the Slabodka Ghetto. For Jews, merely getting there was extremely risky, and this fact alone strengthened the ranks of the skeptics and the weight of their doubts: Was the whole idea of preparing to join the partisans really a trick that would only hasten the destruction of the ghetto? And then there was the gnawing, heartbreaking question: What would happen to the children? And the elderly? The well-known Jewish devotion to family did not permit an easy or frivolous answer to that question.

No small hindrance to organizing the partisan movement in the Slabodka Ghetto were the various rumors—some of them well-founded—about the attitude of partisans even toward those Jews who had already been accepted into detachments: it was said that Jews were being given the most dangerous assignments and that they were being shot in the back.

Another obstacle was the well-known fact that every partisan had to take an oath of allegiance to "Comrade Stalin." I personally spoke with more than one Zionist in the Slabodka Ghetto (where Zionists were in the majority) who was ready to join the partisans but could not make peace with his conscience over the loyalty oath he would have to take.

These and other considerations had a powerful effect on the younger Jews in the ghetto. One must remember that in these bleak circumstances, the struggle for national liberation could not inspire an attempt to break through the barbed wire fence and join the partisans. No one in the ghetto would have been so naive as to be "inspired" by such thoughts.

Here another truth must be plainly stated, one that was covered up, for understandable reasons, immediately following World War II: the main reason that Jewish youth fought to get out of the ghettos and into the forest was not in order to take vengeance on the Germans. This may have become the accepted version of all the memoir and history writers of the Jewish partisan movement, and undoubtedly the motive of revenge played a part. But the single most important reason a young Jew went into the forest, the single most important reason all the national Jewish organizations became involved in the partisan movement, was this: to save lives.

In the deepest sense, saving one's own life—even for egotistic reasons—was the best revenge one could take on the murderous Nazis. Killing the enemy, when there were tens of millions of them? That was hardly possible. What could be attempted, though, was to keep as many Jews as possible alive at a time when the Jewish people itself was in danger of extinction. That was the strategy of the leading Jewish agencies in the ghetto.

I recall a meeting of the Socialist-Zionist central committee in the Slabodka Ghetto at which this question was stormily debated. Engraved in my memory are the words of one man who banged on the table and interrupted a speaker: "The guardian angel of our people does not demand of us any dead heroes! He demands only one thing: life! To save the life of one Jew now, more than ever, is to save a whole world. Let us save worlds now, not destroy them—and that will be our revenge! A thousand living Jews will be a greater sanctification of God's name than a thousand Jews dead on the barricades!"

Most of the people in the room endorsed that view. And apparently all the other political parties in the ghetto also conducted their activities in that spirit.

So it would not be true to say that Jews in the ghettos joined the partisans to avenge the Jewish blood that had been shed and perhaps also save themselves from death. No. Young Jews ran from the ghetto to join the partisans in order to save their own lives and in that way perhaps also take revenge on the murderers of their families and the Jewish people as a whole.

In the first stage of organizing the Jewish partisan movement in the Slabodka Ghetto it happened that I was not a passive onlooker, so I can testify that all the discussion around this question in the leading Zionist committee centered on one question: How and in what way could we rescue more Jews from the ghetto? It was not at all on the question of how we could take more revenge on the Germans. Jews from other ghettos, when they are not speaking publicly, will tell you the same thing.

There were three main opinions among the leading underground organizations on the question of how best to save as many Jews as possible in the Slabodka Ghetto (and, of course, in other ghettos too):

(1) Construct a hiding place inside the ghetto itself. In the early days we did not know that the Germans were burning down the

ghettos. And even later, when there were already rumors about such wholesale liquidations of ghettos, many would still not give up the idea of creating a hiding place. Jews in the Slabodka Ghetto who took this approach later perished in the ruins of their own bunkers.

(2) Escape from the ghetto and find shelter with a friendly peasant, or, less safely, simply get out of the ghetto, because one never knew when the hour of liquidation would come. Only a small number of people could take this path. For the organizations this was not even a choice, except in rare instances, such as saving children by hiding them in monasteries or with friendly peasants.

(3) Join the partisans. Those who argued this believed that only in this way would it be possible to establish better communication with the outside world and receive the necessary help and support.

The last two approaches had something in common: they advocated leaving the ghetto. But all three struggled with the same fateful question: When would the moment of liquidation arrive? Understandably, those who believed that creating a hiding place offered the most safety would put off that date for as long as possible. Those who favored leaving the ghetto argued that the sooner we got out the better, without speculating about the date the liquidation would take place.

Nevertheless, human character is always a factor. The same people who had made up their minds to join the partisans or hide with peasants could not always find the courage to do it sooner rather than later. Some of my own friends, who were also thinking of escaping from the ghetto, could not get themselves to give up what the ghetto did provide—temporary security and a roof over one's head. Leaving the ghetto meant immediately risking your life and subjecting yourself to worse conditions. So some people, under various pretexts, kept putting off the moment of decision.

A close friend of mine, who had a good opportunity to leave the ghetto in time, could not find the inner strength to leave the "comforts" (there were some) of the ghetto, and when he did finally decide to act, it was too late.

Another friend tried to hide his weakness with the delusion that he would know in advance when the Germans were preparing to liquidate the ghetto. That too turned out to be self-deception.

My own opinion was that it would be better to get out of the ghetto ten months too early than ten minutes too late. It was better to take the risk now, so that later you might have a chance to save yourself, than to be "safe" for the present and put yourself in danger of being trapped.

Much has already been written about the life of the Jews in ghettos. Much material has also seen the light of day about the Jewish partisan movement during World War II. To all this we may now add a diary of a ghetto refugee written in pig pens, in the wild bushes, and in the Lithuanian forest. In it you will find no battle accounts, no dramatic scenes—only a string of simple, daily experiences under the shadow of the German monster. And that in itself was one long, horror-filled drama.

Because I had no paper at my disposal, these notes were written in a used copybook I found in a Lithuanian butcher's shop. I had to write between the lines, and I made it look like a Hebrew-Yiddish songbook, as you will see from the accompanying photostats. At first, I kept the diary in a disguised form, as though it had been written during the violence in Palestine in 1937. Everything was disguised—dates, names, places. But very soon we lost our naive delusion that this sort of camouflage would lessen our peril should the notes fall into the hands of the Germans. Thereafter, all the events, names, and dates written down were real.

I have edited these notes as little as possible. Most of them were written as the events happened or immediately afterward so that as much as possible of the hot breath of the actual experience would remain.

But there was an even more important reason: 99 percent of the time the author's chance of surviving the Holocaust was zero, so the diary is really a sort of last will and testament—and is one permitted to change a will?

CHAPTER 1

Escape From The Barbed Wire

OCTOBER 20, 1943

After lengthy preparations and several failures, we finally succeeded in getting out of the Slabodka Ghetto. This time a peasant was waiting with his wagon exactly on time at an isolated spot on the outskirts of Kovno.

Who can possibly convey the anguish of a person who is about to take a life-or-death leap? We will have to cover forty kilometers before we reach our hiding place in Karalgaris, near Vilkija. How many times will death be lying in wait for us?

For the first part of the journey, we all kept the yellow patches on our backs and chests, and it seemed that any moment someone would stop us. When we finally removed those "Jewish insignia," we could still feel fingers pointing at us from all sides as if to shout: "There are Jews traveling."

With that feeling of dread there is the constant wish to arrive somewhere: to crawl into a hole, to be enclosed between walls . . . anywhere just so long as we no longer see any human beings and they don't see us.

Human beings?

We are still only twelve kilometers from Kovno, at Raudondvaris Hill. (Jews used to call it "Red Courtyard," a literal translation of the Lithuanian name.) Dusk has fallen, but it is still quite light. Are we mistaken, or is that a group of German soldiers at the bottom of the hill? No, we are not mistaken. They are the "best kind" of Germans—Gestapo. Apparently they had trouble with their car. We gather up all our courage—the courage of people sentenced to death—and as we ride past we greet them with a loud, hearty "Good day!"

We pass by peacefully.

What was our pulse rate during those few seconds?

The darker the night grows, the brighter our spirits become. Children of a people who "brought light unto the nations" now seek protection from the dark . . .

But this does not always work. Suddenly the darkness is pierced by a cry of pain: "Oh! Help me!" Crossing a small bridge our wagon overturned, pinning my wife under a wheel. We manage to drag her out with only a badly bruised arm. Is it broken? While this is going on we are suddenly attacked by a pack of dogs from a nearby cottage. Our peasant driver loses his temper:

"Keep your voices down! Germans often visit that house!"

So we smother our fears, grit our teeth, and keep perfectly quiet until we pass through this new danger zone.

We have been traveling this remote Lithuanian road for about ten hours. We are now plodding through the deep mud of a half-frozen October night. For the horse, every step is forty pounds, and very frequently he gets stuck. The road seems endless, but the driver keeps reassuring us: "Just one more kilometer." We have already traveled ten of these "one more" kilometers.

The driver lands another blow: "Could I have taken the wrong turn?" he wonders aloud. "Looks like we might have to stay here till morning."

Our spirits sink even lower. This is all we needed. The driver gets off the wagon to survey the area. Waiting for him to return is an eternity, and serious suspicions enter our minds. A peasant who had lived in these parts all his life, who knows every hidden path blindfolded . . . suddenly he discovers he has lost his way? Have we fallen into a trap? Has the driver in fact gone to get the rest of his gang so they can finish us all off right here?

But the driver returns alone. A rock rolls off our hearts. "We're on the right road," he tells us. "We'll be there very soon." Precisely because we had just been having such terrible thoughts about him he has now become positively beautiful to us.

We ride along narrow roads that twist and turn between bushes and stunted trees. For hundreds of meters we ride through water so deep that we are afraid of drowning. The trees are so short that their branches scratch our faces. We seem to be getting nowhere. But the peasant is a good driver, and after a few more hours of bumping and bouncing we can see a feeble light in the distance.

"That's my house," the peasant announces.

Our hearts are singing. This is how a man must feel when he gets a last-minute reprieve from the gallows. When we reach the house an old, shriveled peasant woman is there to greet us. "I was afraid they had shot you," she says to her husband. She kisses my wife and my sister-in-law with real affection. "Here you'll be treated like my own children."

The women burst into tears. I can barely refrain from crying myself. My heart almost stops at this extraordinary sight: a complete stranger, embracing and kissing two Jewish women! In these days!

OCTOBER 21

The morning after our first night in the barn we examine our new "home." The whole cottage, with its leaky straw roof, consists of one room in which the peasant couple cook, eat, and sleep. There is no floor. In the center of the room there is a large patch of damp clay where they have recently covered over a hole. The walls are black with soot. There is no chair, no table. The bed, knocked together out of four boards, has no sheet, no pillow. The oven occupies a quarter of the room. When it's burning, smoke oozes out of all its cracks. At night the room is lit by pine splinters that the couple light one after the other. The "sink" is a trough for washing your face, feet, dirty clothes—and for kneading dough. The eating utensils consist of one fork, one knife, one spoon, and a bowl that is shared with the pig. Also sharing this space is an emaciated black and white cat and a hen who has a blue, naked backside instead of feathers.

This is a way of life that must have been common centuries ago. How long are we fated to live it?

Our rescuer is around seventy but still strong. This is his third war. In the Russo-Japanese War and in World War I he served on many fronts. He has married off four sons and two daughters, but now they want nothing to do with him. He has grandchildren, but he doesn't even know what they look like. "Children are only good when they're young," he tells us caustically. He is a hardened man, like the piece of barren land around his cottage. His main support, his nag, collapsed two weeks ago, but our host is still in good spirits, with a rhyming joke for every occasion. His pipe is hardly ever out of his mouth. His present wife, his second, appears to be in her sixties. In contrast to him, she is weak and bony—a "broken vessel," he calls her.

The most important living creature here is the dog, Lapyuk. He is tied to the house by a rope. For us, his every bark is a signal—go hide! We have exchanged our life in a city filled with people for a dog and a forest. We have traveled from the 20th century back to the Dark Ages.

We, with our soap and our toothpaste, our books and our pens—here in this wild cottage. Two different worlds. Which is better?

OCTOBER 23

The little bit of bread we brought with us has been consumed. The old couple, Tadeusz and Barbora, scurry around trying to find us something to eat. This can arouse suspicion: Since when has this old couple needed so much bread? And why are they risking their lives for us, people they are meeting for the first time?

Tadeusz says: "Why didn't you put up a fight? It might have been better for you. I like that Jew from Keidan who killed two partisans and wounded a third during an action, even though he himself died. That's the way!"

The old woman says: "Wild beasts they are, burying little children alive in ditches—our children are just like yours. So we will take care of you."

Evening. We are all in the cottage. Suddenly the dog starts barking. A loud knock on the window. Tadeusz puts out the light.

"Who's there?" the old woman asks as we tremble in fear.

"Antanas!"

It's the peasant who organized the hiding place here. They light the candle again. The guest comes in with a sack on his shoulders, puts it down on the ground. Food for us. Lest he leave tracks he walked through the swamp, all the way in the dark, rather than come by horse from his house, which is four kilometers away. He is soaked to the skin and muddy all over. Sweat runs down his face, which has signs of fear on it but also satisfaction, because he is doing a good deed at the risk of his own life. He absolutely refuses to accept money from us for the food.

How could one even begin to compare him and our old couple to those Lithuanian partisans?

OCTOBER 24

It is only our fourth day here, and already the time drags. What will it be like later?

During the day we stay in the stable, which is locked from inside. Every step we hear outside unnerves us. Every rustle hammers our hearts. We hear voices of boys and girls at play. Farmers pasturing their cows. The tinkling little bells that the animals wear around their necks fill the air with good cheer. We peer through the cracks in the stall, praying that no one discovers us. A song tugs maddeningly at the heartstrings: "Bells are ringing somewhere far away . . ."

The pain in my wife's arm and the contrast between the sun and fields outside and darkness and the stench inside depresses her. "Let's go back to the ghetto," Raja says. "Whatever will happen to everyone else there will happen to us."

In the evening the mood grows a little more relaxed. The old man brought home a piglet, and naturally it moved in with us. Our new neighbor keeps squealing to high heaven, giving us all a headache. But at the same time this dispels the leaden silence that hangs over the stable. The feeling that there is still a living, breathing world out there is somehow encouraging.

The most important thing for our safety is that no stranger

should ever set eyes on us. The moment a neighbor finds out about us, our hiding place is kaput. The only creature able to safeguard us from any surprises is the dog. But sometimes even a dog dozes off, as happened today. Our loyal watchman had not even managed to bark once before a stranger already had his hand on the doorknob—and we happened to be in the house at the time. The old woman ran to the door all out of breath. Pale as death, she blocked the doorway. We heard a man's voice.

"Where's Tadeusz?"

"Out."

"I'll come in and wait for him."

"Not now."

"Why not?"

"There's a sick woman in here."

"A woman? What woman?"

"A Gypsy. She was passing by."

During the conversation we quietly try to hide in the room itself. One of us crawls under the bed. A second one climbs up on top of the oven and covers herself with rags. A third crawls inside the big oven.

Is this the story my dear mother used to tell us about children who hide from a bear, or a witch, when they are alone in the house? No, this is not a story. It is a game of death. This time, fortunately, it has a happy ending. The man accepts the explanation and leaves.

An evening of expectations. Today five other Jews are supposed to arrive. We do not go to bed in the stable but remain inside the cottage. The hours are as long as years. We grow more and more uneasy because they should have arrived long ago. The old woman says: "Who knows what could have happened to them? It's already midnight." We lie down on the hard bench, but the uneasiness and the fleas make it impossible to close our eyes. Even the old woman cannot fall asleep, so she sits down at her weaving loom. Her bony fingers run monotonously over the thread. What time is it now? Who knows? How many Jews in the ghetto still have their watches?

At every sound we prick up our ears. Maybe. Maybe.

Suddenly the dog starts barking. Are they here? A prearranged knock on the window pane. The signal.

Who can describe the joy? When was a friendly kiss so emotional?

A light in a poor peasant cottage at such a late hour can arouse suspicion. We quickly cross over into the barn. The talking will have to wait until tomorrow.

OCTOBER 25

A more cheerful mood. Five more Jews is no trivial matter. We tell each other news of the ghetto, news of friends, of the world "out there." Our old Tadeusz, who is listening to our talk, notices for the first time that his little cottage has suddenly filled up with eight living Jews—he must have felt as if his brain had grown too crowded. He breaks into our conversation. "Where am I going to put you all?"

One of us tries to anticipate him: "Well, we'll try to find another place and divide ourselves up."

To which he replies: "Yes, yes, but there aren't that many good people around here."

As he says this, he bends his head and tamps down the tobacco in his pipe. With a faint smile that is quickly clouded over by the deep furrows in his face, he says: "We'll manage somehow. Almost all of you are young. You still have a life to live. I'm not doing this for the money. I'm pretty old myself. I won't take the money with me to my grave. I just don't want to see any more innocent blood spilled. If I could, I would save more Jews. But since I can't, I'll protect those that I can. I want to show you that not all Lithuanians are like those partisans of ours. I happened to be in Ariogala when they led the Jews there to the slaughter. The Jews really believed what they were told: that they were being taken out to work. But in fact they were taken to the Dubysa River. When they saw the graves that had been dug there for them, they threw down their bundles and started screaming and crying. It's a wonder the earth didn't split open. I cracked the whip for my horse to go and put my hands over my ears like many other peasants there did. I will never forget that scene. And I will do everything I can at least to prevent that from happening to you."

We all looked at each other with the same question in our eyes: "How many Jews would have been capable of such a thing?"

OCTOBER 26

The area around here could have been created especially for Jews escaping from the ghetto. Swamps and bushes and woods. Dense woods and sparse villages. That's the greatest virtue of our surroundings. The closest neighbor is some two hundred meters away, concealed by trees of all sizes.

Very rarely do you see a living person. The only regular passerby is a peasant woman with wooden milk pails. Every morning around seven she delivers milk from her own and neighboring farms to a nearby estate. She does this under orders from the German authorities. Before we came she would stop by here every morning. The old woman would come out to meet her and invite her into the house. But now the old woman has somehow managed to keep her outside, which might in itself eventually arouse suspicion. So she told us today that tomorrow morning we must clean up every last crumb in the house because she wants to invite the milk woman in. Let her see that everything is the way it has always been . . .

OCTOBER 27

Life goes on even when you hear the sound of death's wings fluttering over you every minute of the day and night.

Without any previous discussion a certain order has established itself in our daily existence. The older couple in our group, Mr. and Mrs. F, act as if they were the lord and lady of the manor. They sleep in the house, lay around all day in their pajamas, and generally do things that simply invite trouble for us all.

We talk with them over and over about these simple and easily understandable matters—and still they do not change their habits. Even at the edge of the abyss the confused Babel of languages goes on.

OCTOBER 28

It is two years to the day since the horror of the "Great Action." We live with terrible feelings of revenge, of hate and grief. Here in this dirty stable, we feel it even more sharply, more deeply.

We started a conversation with old Tadeusz about that action. He offers his opinion: "I can understand it when soldiers fight for their positions. But to go out and murder women and children—only cowardly cutthroats could do that." He takes a long pull on his pipe and sinks into thought.

A sudden crackle of gunfire silences us. Where is it coming from? Gunfire in such a remote area? The dog starts barking hysterically. Faces turn white as chalk. The silence is deadly. That same morning old Barbora had told us the police were looking for Gypsies and Poles in our neighborhood. Are we in a trap?

This time it ends peacefully, but in each one of us the determination grows to build some sort of hiding place so that the Germans will at least not be able to catch us in the first few moments of their arrival.

The old man brings us another piece of news: "They have driven several thousand more Jews out of the ghetto." On the 28th of October! Can this be true?

OCTOBER 29

We are trying to build a hiding place in the hay. From the nearby woods we have brought branches and tree trunks, and with them we weave a wall, with a hole at the bottom for entrance and exit. We cover the hole with hay.

It's not such a wonderful place to hide, but it does provide some feeling of safety. After all, the naiveté of childhood never completely disappears, especially in moments of mortal peril.

Today we have started a system of keeping watch. For four hours during the day the three younger men will be on duty. Through the cracks they will be looking for any signs of movement in the general area.

I take the first watch. All the others are in the hiding place inside the barn. I am busy staring through the cracks. Outside are workers on threshing machines, singing while they work. Only a few steps away it's a beautiful world, while we—children of the Chosen People—are lying in a living grave.

Suddenly he comes into my view—a man carrying a briefcase. He is entering the cottage. An extremely unusual sight for this neighborhood. As unusual as the sight of an automobile was in a Lithuanian village forty years ago. As soon as he leaves the house, the old woman runs in and tells us that the village elder was here. He told her that he could speak only to the "man of the house," which meant it was a very important matter. Was it about us? A very alarming development.

When the old man comes home he goes looking for the man with the briefcase. It turns out that the elder had really needed him urgently: he needed a barrel for some whisky he had made at home. We listen to the old man's story and smile. How many such smiles can the human heart endure?

OCTOBER 30

My friend Moyshe, who has just finished his lookout duty, brings me a "treasure." Not having anything else to do, he has written a poem. I stare at him incredulously. Since when has he been writing poetry? In normal times he had been as lacking in imagination as a stick of wood.

I read the first few lines. If I were an editor, it would have gone right into the wastebasket. But how many Yiddish poems were created in a pig pen? Perhaps I should record it here as a remembrance of the Destruction.

> In a far corner of the Lithuanian land
> I stand on watch with a rifle in my hand.
> A gathering of Jews,
> Only eight souls
> Guarding against death by men of hate.
> They guard us—our two sentinels—he is seventy and sixty is she.
> And their dog, he too stands guard, as does the vast

dense forest.

Two old people with the blood of heroes.
Who hate the Kubiliūnas killers.
Out of righteousness they further weave
The human dream of friendliness to Jews.

CHAPTER 2

In The House And In The Stable

NOVEMBER 1

Today we noticed that several of us were missing some personal belongings. Since both of our protectors happened to be away that day, we made a quick inspection of the house. To our amazement we found the missing socks, a lead pencil, two handkerchiefs, and a few other such items.

Who can understand the human soul? Harboring strangers at the risk of their own lives and still unable to resist the pilfering of a handkerchief!

Old Tadeusz, who had been in Tsaikiszok [now known as Čekiškė], brings us news that the Germans have taken some seven thousand Jews out of the Slabodka Ghetto. We had heard similar reports before. Apparently, this terrible news is correct. A gallery of friends and acquaintances passes before our eyes . . . and our hearts break. We all grow exceedingly despondent.

NOVEMBER 3

The first indirect "greetings" from other Jews. The wife of the man who supplied the horse that brought us here tells us that two Jews from the ghetto came to her house and asked about us. They also brought a note from our dear friend Isaac Srebnitsky, a leading activist in the ghetto. In his note he tells us that the situation in the ghetto is growing worse day by day and that we must help him and his wife Sonia get out. The date for our reply is given as November 2nd—and we did not receive his note until the 3rd! What to do now? How can we reach him?

For reasons of "security" the woman did not send the two Jews to us but gave them the address of another peasant whom she considers trustworthy.

NOVEMBER 4

Antanas, the only non-Jew who knows about our hiding place, and who offered his horses to bring us here, came to see us this evening. He brought with him a wagonload of food—meat, flour, fat—which should last us for six or seven weeks. A veritable fortune!

Today we suffered our first major setback. Mrs. F took sick and had to stay in the house during the day with Tamara to take care of her. On his own initiative, Moyshe also went into the house to help. Suddenly a stranger passed by the window. The dog was asleep on the job apparently, and a strong wind carried off the echo of the stranger's footsteps.

The two women managed to climb up on the oven and cover themselves. Moyshe had no other alternative but to lie down on the bench and feign sleep. Barbora ran to head off the uninvited guest, who happened to be a neighbor.

"Who's that?" he wanted to know, pointing to the bench.

"A passerby."

"One of us?"

"Yes."

The guest's eyes fell on the good boots of the sleeping "passerby," but all he said was "Hm-m-m."

We were all shaken by this incident and began discussing plans to flee. But where to? Without an answer to that question we have no choice but to stay where we are.

NOVEMBER 7

Several days passed uneventfully and we began to feel relieved. A big celebration today. The old man brought us a note from M's brother, who lives in Kovno under Lithuanian identification papers. A toast with vodka even added a festive note.

Today the first snow fell, leaving a white coat of innocence all around us. How much joy the snow once brought to Jewish children in the Lithuanian towns! The first snowfall here—how much pain and sadness it now inflicts upon our hearts . . .

NOVEMBER 8

Dreams now occupy a prominent place in our lives. None of us ever had as many dreams as we do now. Most of them revolve around the ghetto. We dream about escaping from the ghetto or about returning to the ghetto. We are chased, we run, we are shot at. It's not unusual for us to cry out in our sleep.

Today old Tadeusz made a long speech to us: "Mr. F did many favors for Antanas. Mr. F gave him thirty-seven acres of land and many valuable belongings for safekeeping. Now Antanas wants to return the favor and save your lives. But he is putting me in danger, not himself. Before you came here, Antanas told me: 'You'll benefit from it, too. I'll give you my cow to pasture. Mr. F will come here from the ghetto with his horse and wagon, which you can keep for yourself.' But I don't want you to think I'm risking my life for money. I've already lived my seventy years—what can I gain and what can I lose? I'm not afraid of dying—life isn't worth all that much anyway. But with a horse, life is still a little better, and at my age a person wants to take it a little easier."

The old man is unquestionably right. We have already talked about this among ourselves. We are afraid of just two things: Firstly, a horse will gradually eat up all the hay, which is our only protection now, our only hiding place. And secondly, the neighbors may get suspicious. When did old Tadeusz inherit such a fortune?

NOVEMBER 12

The weather is growing colder and colder. Not all of us are prepared for it. All we had been concerned with was getting our bodies out of there. For some of us, that was the most we could do. But Mr. F, who once owned property in this part of the country, was practical enough to prepare for winter. He has six warm blankets, but as for offering one to someone who has none—forget it! He has big fur coats—and keeps them in a closet for the mice. Mr. F, whom we call "the Squire," said that after liberation he would leave all his things to Antanas. But now he can't bear the thought of offering a blanket to his fellow Jews who are, just like him, trying to save their lives and are suffering terribly from the cold.

NOVEMBER 14

A suicide. One of the local farmers did not get back a sum of money that he had lent to a neighbor, so he hanged himself. The whole village is in an uproar, both because the event was such a rare one in these parts and because the priest refused to perform the last rites and the body has already been held for four days. Irate, the old man talks to us about this. "How can they do that—refuse to bury a person? He was a human being like anyone else, and he has that right."

The old woman has a different opinion. "He took his own life, so let the worms eat him. And if he really had no other choice but to hang himself, then let him go out in the woods and hang himself. Let him not bring shame and disgrace on his family."

"Shut your mouth!" the old man cut in. "What is he—a murderer, a robber, a gangster? He hurt only himself, cut his own life short. Whose business is that?"

The old woman raises her eyes to heaven. "But the Holy Scriptures—"

Again he doesn't let her finish. "Ech! Fairy tales! Something to fool the public with so they can raise money. Nobody was ever up there in heaven, and no one knows the management up there. Sometimes I go to the priest for confession—but if I don't feel like it, I won't." He spits on the floor, rolls his watery eyes, and that's the end of the religious-philosophical disquisition.

That's our protector. Is primitive atheism in our circumstances better than pious Catholicism?

NOVEMBER 17

Several quiet days. Minor scares. A strange passerby. The dog barks. Nothing more. Thank God for that.

Days at a time we lie around in the barn. A good part of the day we sleep—less time to think. I have trouble sleeping during the day, however, so all day long I stand guard at the cracks in the barn door, my eyes focused on the door of the cottage.

In these cold and long hours, breakfasts and lunches are a welcome relief. The early hours of the day drag and drag, stretching like tar. Each hour a year. But after lunch it's not so bad. Between four and five o'clock it grows dark, and you can sneak into the house for a little while to warm up your bones. In the final daylight hours, everyone moves out of the hay hole and takes up positions at the cracks in the barn door. We therefore call the twilight hours Neilah.

Because of the increasing cold, two or three persons sleep in the house every night. Sometimes it happens that a rare visitor comes late at night or very early in the morning, when we are still asleep. During those hours the dog's sense of hearing is especially keen, and the people in the cottage have time to disappear on top of the oven or up in the attic. But they must be sure to take all their clothing and shoes with them, because the least thing out of place in such a forsaken corner of the world arouses suspicion.

One of these unwelcome visits almost resulted in catastrophe. Hearing the loud barking of the dog, Raja climbed up on the oven and pulled a coat over herself. The ovens are built so that one part can be used for storing pots and pans as well as for sleeping. The oven happened to be very hot at that time because they had baked bread that day. The visitor meanwhile sat and told story after story.

Another ten minutes and Raja, hiding up there on the oven, would have been unable to endure the heat any longer. When the visitor left and she finally came down, all bathed in perspiration, she fell to the ground in a dead faint.

NOVEMBER 19

Rain, snow, slush. Dreary days. The woods are bare and gloomy. The dog huddles in the hay. Chickens tramp around in the loft. Lizards with their long colorful tails, something we never see in the city, desperately seek shelter from the cold. A Lithuanian autumn in the countryside. Sad. Depressing. Haunting.

Suddenly a violent storm. Can the barn withstand it? The beams are tottering. The pyramid-shaped haystacks outside shake from side to side as if they are about to topple over. The old man has reinforced the roof over the cottage with heavy logs.

Inside the barn we are terrified. One more minute of this hammering by the storm and we'll all be buried alive if the barn doesn't hold up. At dusk, earlier than our usual practice, we sneak into our "palace" one at a time, all hunched over, as if we could make ourselves invisible. The dog keeps barking. The wild, elemental force is making fearful noises. The atmosphere is so sinister that we huddle together by the big oven, and in the darkness we start singing a tune quietly, very quietly, so that the storm won't hear the sounds and carry them away to places of abomination.

Out of one tune a second is born, and a third—familiar, poignant songs that remind you of so much and make you feel so hopeless. Before your eyes pass scenes of the Jewish shtetl in Lithuania—parents, friends, those killed in military forts and those who died in their own beds. They all march past you in your imagination. Romantic years become real again, and the robust Jewish life of long past seems like a golden dream you dreamt hundreds of years ago. In this dreamlike state the nostalgic lines of a song are even more powerful, lines you once sang with so much feeling and wistfulness back in the ghetto.

Ikh vil nokh eyn mol zen mayn heym
Tsi is dort ales vi geven
Ot do der taykh, ot do der boym
Ot do der dakh vos halt zikh koym
Ikh vil aheym . . .

I want to see my home once more, I wonder if it's still the same—
There's the river, there's the tree
There's the roof that's barely attached
I want to go home . . .
Home . . . one more time . . . one more time . . .

In the middle of the song we stop singing. Our strength fails us. The tears flow. From the combination of the elevated mood brought on by music and our tears, a mute prayer is born. How long did it last, this dream of home? A minute? An eternity?

The wind howls mournfully, and again one thinks of a Sabbath twilight in a little Lithuanian prayer house. Around the table Jews are chanting chapters from Psalms. The children find a corner where they can sit and tell each other stories about devils and robbers and wolves, frightening each other so much that they start seeing hordes of otherworldly creatures under the table and evil eyes staring at them from the walls—yet it is so sweet and pleasant to sit there and listen . . . just listen. You want the darkness to go on and on, and you hope that the dull thud of the prayer leader's hand on the lectern, announcing the end of the service, might never come and dispel the magic of that childhood world between the sacred and the profane.

What has happened to all those dear, simple Jews? What has happened to all the study houses and all the prayer houses? What has happened to all those Shloymeles and Moysheles? Where did it all disappear to? Jewish melodies of old, Jewish scenes of old—in an ancient peasant cottage, in a Lithuanian village, on a stormy evening—Jewish fate, fateful Jewishness!

NOVEMBER 20

We have now been here a month. We are wondering whether we did the right thing. In the ghetto Jews still sleep in their own beds. The barbed wire is a sort of protection. Here we face death every moment. We live in unspeakable conditions. But developments in the ghetto during this last month seem to justify our decision. The original question that tormented every Jew in the Kovno Ghetto now faces everyone there relentlessly: "Will the ghetto in Kovno remain an exception?" Aside from the inveterate optimists, whose number is greater than one might expect, most Jews in the Slabodka Ghetto believed that the ghetto there would eventually be liquidated. The sharpest difference of opinion arose around the question of timing—"When will this take place?"—and, therefore, "When should we begin preparing the means to escape?"

Almost everyone finally understood that armed self-defense meant suicide. On the fateful question of how to save oneself, there were two choices: 1. To remain safe for today (by staying in the ghetto) and gamble on tomorrow (hoping to get out before the axe falls).

2. To gamble on today (by escaping) in order to be safe tomorrow.

I chose the second way. Now it is thirty days since I acted on my decision—a bitter "period of mourning" during which we all miss terribly the friends and comrades who are now "protected" by the barbed wire.

NOVEMBER 21

In honor of our one-month anniversary, we had a "guest" today. Something fell from the hay in the attic and landed on one of the women sleeping in the stable.

Startled, she jumped up, and we turned on our flashlight. A mouse. In the good old days the women would have begun screaming to high heavens. But now—*sh-sh-sh*. No doubt that tiny creature is not the only one of its kind here.

NOVEMBER 22

Our only living "non-Jewish" neighbor in the barn is . . . the pig. And since one cannot think about death twenty-four hours a day we spend some time admiring the little pig.

This most disgusting creature for Jews, which the old man bought with our money a few weeks ago, thankfully is growing nicely. From seven or eight kilos it's grown to half of a centner.

The old man has explained to us how we can entertain ourselves with this unclean animal. If you take a stick and scratch him with it, he becomes so ecstatic that he'll stretch out to his full length, hold up his head, close his eyes in pleasure, and grunt in sheer delight. As soon as you stop scratching him, he will turn over, offering you his unscratched side, and his eyes will plead with you: "More, more . . ." When he is completely satisfied, he will do a little dance and roll over.

The one drawback is that the pig moves around too much and uses his snout to create havoc—digging up garbage and, when his stomach starts objecting, squealing out loud like a grown-up hog.

To eliminate this desire, Tadeusz today performed an operation on the pig. He pierced the animal's nose and hung a piece of bent wire through it. But just our luck—the operation is not completely successful. The wire is too soft and the snout is too hard. So the old man says to me: "Berelis, sit on him and hold him down."

Just the right one to ask—a Jew from Telšiai, a person who has trouble even looking at a pig. And he wants me to sit down on it and grab hold of its filthy body while the animal is squealing his head off.

Noticing my discomfort, the old man waves his hand disparagingly, sits down hard on the pig's back, pierces the nose with an awl, and pulls the wire through.

Now the pig lies down peacefully, and we can all get some rest.

NOVEMBER 23

With our arrival the need for more firewood in the cottage obviously increased. Fortunately, we are near woods. But Tadeusz cannot carry all that wood back by himself, so we begin going out to the woods with him. This was not as simple as it sounds. We had to give the problem a lot of thought. What if a stranger sees? We solved that problem by relying on a miracle. How many miracles have already occurred to the eight of us even before we got here? So we now become "pioneers." We put on peasant clothing, and as soon as darkness sets in we go out into the woods, about a kilometer or two away. The road is so muddy that your feet get stuck and you can barely pull them out. Despite that, each of us picks up three or four logs and—presto!—mission accomplished. In the cottage we now have a lot of work to do—chopping and sawing the logs. The old man can't stand watching us chop with both hands. He takes over, and even with his seventy years he does the work much more quickly than we can. It's a matter of the right tools. His saw, for example, or his axe—when has a Jew ever been seen with such tools? With his saw, even I am a master craftsman.

As we chop the wood, someone says "*hachshara*"—the preparation for emigration to Israel and subsequent life in kibbutzim. Another responds: "Who knows for what? For the Land of Israel or for the God of Israel?"

If we can still kid around like this, it's a good sign. We still have enough spiritual strength to put up a fight against the death that lies in wait for us.

NOVEMBER 24

A major misfortune: Our dog has disappeared. Terrible nervousness and anxiety, not only among us but also among our protectors. All our activity up to now depended on this "Guardian of Israel," as we affectionately called the dog. When moving from the barn to the house, even when just talking to each other, we had to listen for his signal. A bark meant "Careful! Run and hide! Be quiet!"

All day long we've been talking about the dog. For us it's a matter of life and death.

Today we learned from Tadeusz about some unexpected news he had heard on the radio. News about German defeats. The old man adds that since the battle fronts were moving closer to us, the underground partisan groups in the area were again beginning to organize.

The situation among the Lithuanians is very complicated, however. They want to get rid of the Germans, but they don't like the Russians either. When the reality is unpleasant, one nourishes oneself with fantasy. The Lithuanians are now holding on for dear life to the legend that Sweden will soon enter the war and occupy Lithuania. They have already "heard" about a Lithuanian government that was set up in Stockholm!

Those who occupy themselves with studying the psychology of the Jews in the ghettos (who often believed the wildest rumors) can learn something from the faith of the Lithuanians in their imminent salvation by the Swedes.

This business with Sweden brings to mind the question: Would the Jews in the ghettos (and later in the concentration camps) have been able to survive without the various impossible fantasies and miraculous thousand-and-one-nights stories that fell like hailstones upon their heads in their living graves?

It seems to me the answer to that question is: no. In that suffocating atmosphere of death, all these unbelievable stories were one of the main factors that fortified the courage of the despairing, reinforced the faith of the optimists, and was a real tonic of life for the inhabitants of all the valleys of death.

Thus, we too, in our pig pen—and probably hundreds of others in similar conditions—would have found it much more difficult to survive those many death-or-life months if the most extravagant fantasies had not come to our aid. If we were faced with the reality only, we could not have held out even for a short time.

Without dreams and fantasies and legends it is much more difficult for a Jew to survive in the camps, in the ghettos, in the bunkers.

NOVEMBER 25

Can we be certain that we will be able to hold out here until liberation? This question was raised today by one of our group.

We are discussing plans for the future. We all agree with the opinion expressed by one of the friends: namely, that our situation could grow perilous because we know absolutely nothing about the surrounding terrain. We are not oriented in any particular direction, and we have no connections with any neighbors who might turn out to be trustworthy. We also talked about finding a way to get to the Lithuanian partisans, but in that alternative lies an even greater danger. There are both communist and nationalist partisan groups among the Lithuanians; they fight each other, and both groups are full of provocateurs. Even their central committees are infiltrated, and more than once it has proved damaging to them. There was a rumor that even the underground Lithuanian partisan newspaper, *I Laisvė,* is being published by the Gestapo itself!

The danger in lying holed up in this stable—even though it has advantages—was soon made very clear. A neighbor showed up (the dog was no longer there to warn us) while the old woman was washing the lunch dishes. Peasant women don't stand on ceremony. The neighbor asked her immediately: "Since when do you have so many dishes? Whose boots are those? Whose briefcase is that?"

And as if that weren't enough, she asked another innocent question: "I heard someone talking in the barn—who is in there?"

Was this curious neighbor convinced by the answer she received—that she must have heard Gypsies talking? And what of her other questions—questions from a woman who happened to be there only accidentally? We begin to feel as if the ground is burning under our feet . . .

NOVEMBER 26

Today we have an honored guest—Antanas's wife, Stasia. She tells us that several kilometers from here there are two other Jews in hiding.

She has promised one of the Jews to bring him his sweetheart, who is working in a city brigade. For this favor he has promised Stasia five gold fivers. But the old woman in our group, the former "plutocrat" Mrs. F, talked her out of doing it. The whole enterprise was not safe, she argued. First of all, it is very difficult to contact the Jews in the city brigade, and secondly, the young man cannot even pay her for the risk she would be taking, even if her efforts should prove successful. In short, for some reason that is not clear to me, here was a Jewish woman preventing the rescue of another Jew.

After all this, how should we regard our peasant and his wife, who know only too well what will happen to them if they are caught?

Hurrah! Something we can really celebrate! Our dog has reappeared! In honor of the occasion his masters bring him into the house. We all make a fuss over him. Tadeusz explains to us that this is "dog season"—the dogs are mating—and that they usually spend a few days together with their mates. When have city Jews ever valued a dog so highly as we do now?

NOVEMBER 27

Something new in our stall: a bench. For us it's a very important piece of furniture. We were used to losing the use of our feet from standing all day. This will make eating, too, a bit easier and tidier. We're used to eating on our laps, on the ground, on the trough between us and the pig.

In time we'll get so used to being here that we won't have any desire to leave.

NOVEMBER 28

Tadeusz returned today from his trip to the market day in Tsaikiszok. Even before he had closed the door behind him, he asked us: "Hey, fellows, do you have any weapons?"

We looked at him with a combination of suspicion and surprise. This is the first time he ever asked us such a question. Why today?

He deliberately delayed his reply, making us more and more curious. He took his time about unharnessing the horse he had borrowed. Finally, he raised his eyes and said: "You're a bunch of misfits! These days you need to know how to fire a gun, you understand? Listen to this. On the way back I gave one of our people a lift, and this is what he told me. Not far from Tsaikiszok something happened. Three of your people were hiding with a partisan. After a whole year passed, the partisan got tired of the whole business and went to the police. Your people had guns, so they opened fire and escaped.

"The partisan was afraid to come back into his own house. The Jews might come back and take revenge. For three weeks he wandered around in strange villages, sleeping in strange beds. But the three Jews kept their eye on him, and one night when he came home to sleep, they broke in, killed him, and set fire to the house."

The old man was silent for a few moments as he watched our faces. Then, with a mischievous smile, he added: "Now *that's* something I understand! I really do!"

NOVEMBER 29

First results of not bathing for a month and sleeping almost every night in the hay with your clothes on: in the straw there are fleas, big ones, and they make your life miserable. When they bite you, you jump. These detestable little creatures are especially bad when there's a change in the weather. And they have a special weakness for clean underwear. The first night in fresh underwear it's almost impossible to sleep.

The third of Pharaoh's plagues is also making itself felt. The lice in these parts grow to an unusual size. Who knows what will happen later, and how we shall be able to cope with them if our living conditions don't get any better?

CHAPTER 3

Dangers And Nightmares

NOVEMBER 30

Tadeusz has finally bought himself a horse. A fine horse. Tadeusz came riding up on it today like a proud aristocrat, his face shining with pleasure. In the last few years two horses have died on him, one after the other. For more than a year now he has been without a horse, so acquiring another one was his dream.

We are happy for him, although we're afraid the new horse might arouse suspicion among his neighbors, who would then start telling stories that could prove dangerous for us. It is a terrible thing to live like thieves, constantly looking over your shoulder for the police.

Today the old man also brought along a new dog that he found wandering on the road. Using pieces of bread as bait, he had no problem getting the dog to follow him home. A truly beautiful animal, big as a wolf. With good training, he could become an excellent sentry for us.

DECEMBER 1

The old man is making all the necessary preparations in the barn for the horse. There are plenty of things to do because the entire barn, our present home, is a flimsy piece of work, and if the horse should ever decide to pull hard at his chain in here the whole structure would collapse. We are pleased that he is making the barn a safer place, supporting it on all sides with heavy logs. Moreover, on account of the horse, the old man has removed the pig.

The new boarder did present us with a new problem, however. No doubt the neighbors will come round to admire Tadeusz's new acquisition. Our presence in the "salon"—the front part of the stable, plus our baskets of food stored there, could become another threat to our safety.

DECEMBER 4

Our apprehensiveness soon proved to be justified. The night happened to be a very cold one. Six of us had slipped into the house to warm up. It wasn't long before a neighbor showed up to offer his congratulations. We rushed to the rickety ladder and quickly climbed up to the attic. More of the straw-covered roof is exposed than is protected. The wind blew in from all directions and we dared not move a muscle, since every movement can be heard below, where our guest is sitting. We console ourselves with the hope that the visit will be a short one. Instead the dog starts barking—another guest is arriving.

Our hands start to freeze; our feet feel even worse. All of us are beginning to turn blue. But we must be as motionless as statues. The guests show no sign of leaving. Even worse, two more have arrived, and the whole company goes back to the barn to inspect the new horse. Afterward they come right back to the house.

The women can no longer feel their own feet. Their teeth are chattering. Four hours in the cold without moving! Finally the guests leave. Half frozen, we get as close to the hot oven as we can.

The old man tells us that one of the guests has taken the old dog home with him. He explains that it might arouse talk for him to own two dogs. He is correct, of course. But we had gotten so accustomed to Lapyuk, who saved us from more than one misfortune, that his absence saddens us. We all wish him the best of luck in his dog's life—may it be better than ours . . .

DECEMBER 7

This day is the forty-ninth that we are here, like the seven weeks following the offering of the Omer. After the customary counting of the sad days between Passover and Shavuot, the holiday of the Giving of the Torah arrives, the happy day of Shavuot and its greenery. What will come after our forty-nine dreadful days in a strange place among kind-hearted but complete strangers? The melancholy of those who count the Omer diminishes with each passing day as they think about the approaching holiday. But counting an Omer to infinity, not seeing any end in sight, or any pattern, not knowing whether you will ever again experience the joy of an approaching holiday—that sort of counting is doubly difficult and doubly bitter . . .

Nevertheless, you still feel a little better when the day passes into the abyss of forgetting, and the time remaining until our liberation—if we ever live to see that day—does grow shorter. So we count the days here and are happy to see each one end, as the days become weeks and the weeks are already becoming months.

It is in this harrowing situation that I have come to better understand the deep meaning of sefira, the counting of the Omer, which in my childhood years we would so hastily slip through our teeth, often combining more than one day. Jewish customs . . . how much more dear they become in hours of shattering experiences, in times of grievous last confessions.

DECEMBER 8

Today a guest told the old man the following story. Near Srednik, two white-clad men attacked a woman and her child. The child ran away and alerted some peasants, who told the local police. They searched the area and in a cave in the woods found three armed Jews with the woman they had captured. She was still alive. The peasants said that Jews who have escaped from the ghetto roam the forest in order to attack Christians, thereby avenging the blood of their families. Such stories, which seem to have no basis at all in fact, can become a danger not only to the ghetto but to those Jews who are hiding in the villages and the forest. Apparently they are deliberately being circulated by the local German propagandists in Kovno.

DECEMBER 9

Due to mounting fears of discovery, today we took a risky step. In the evening Tamara and Shlomo went to Antanas's house without telling Tadeusz. Their task was to look for another possible hiding place and also to get to know the location of the roads in the area.

Our prayers went with them.

Our hosts found out and were quite disturbed by this drastic step that we took without asking their opinion. "We're protecting you every step of the way," they argued, "and here you've gone and sent people out on roads that even old settlers like us get lost on, especially at night. You are endangering not only yourselves but us too."

When the two scouts returned, it turned out that the two old folks were absolutely right. On the way to see Antanas things went smoothly, but coming back they lost their way. For hours they wandered around and around and kept coming back to the same place, as if demons were leading them. They had no other choice but to knock at a window—in the middle of the night!—and ask for directions. This is one of the most dangerous things you can do in an isolated area like this, because the next day everyone in the village will know about it. In one house they were given such a friendly welcome that they were invited in. Their appearance, along with their accent, made it impossible for them not to answer their host's question: "You are Jews?"

Our plan was a mistake that could very well seal our fate, and it took the life out of us such that we were not even interested in hearing details of their adventure. But we did learn that ever since the fourth of this month, masses of Jews were being sent every day from the ghetto to the caserne camps of Shantz, leaving us utterly distraught.

DECEMBER 10

Our fright over the "Columbus voyage of discovery" of our two people was well-founded. The very next morning a neighbor appeared with a story about two people who had stopped at her house and asked directions. "They are not our people," she said, "but they are not strangers either, else how do they know the names of some of the folks around here?"

That afternoon another person showed up with the same story, which meant that the entire neighborhood was already talking about this extraordinary event.

There now hung over our heads a fear of imminent calamity. When troubles begin, they usually come in pairs. One of our two explorers, Shlomo, took sick, no doubt as much a result of the unnerving experience itself as of crawling through the woods. His temperature rose quickly. There was nothing we could do but leave him in the house, in bed, in the middle of the day. Again, we had to depend on a miracle that no one would come to visit.

Today the other scout, Tamara, told me confidentially that in Antanas's house they had met two other Jews. They did not report this to us because they did not want our former Jewish "plutocrat" (Mr. F), whose entire capital is now in Antanas's hands, to become upset and precipitate a commotion; after all, Antanas had refused to take him into his house, but now complete strangers were paying Antanas very heavily, and apparently a heavy coin weighs more than a former friendship with a Jew.

These two strangers must have a lot of money. They are eating well and can't start a meal without a liter of homebrew. They have already exhausted the supply of local fowl: an example of "eat, drink, and be merry, for tomorrow you die." For Jews of this sort, it is obviously easier to survive the years of pestilence and destruction.

DECEMBER 13

I am looking through the crack in the stable door when my ears pick up an unusual sound. Awful screams, inhuman cries. Never in my life have I heard such sounds. They seem to be coming from the cottage. I motion to the others. They confirm my fears. What can it be? Is he beating her? Is he blaming her for all their troubles? Or perhaps we hadn't noticed that strangers have broken into the house and are beating our hosts? Should we try to help?

But suddenly Barbora comes running out the door all excited, her face flushed.

"What is happening?" I ask her.

"Nothing!"

"Nothing?"

"Nothing!" she insists, and she looks at us as if we are the ones who are crazy. She cannot understand why we're so agitated . . .

Incredible. It turns out that in our present state of mind, our nerves are strung so tight that the unusual howling of the wind through the trees sounds to our ears like human screams.

DECEMBER 14

The worst day so far. Around lunchtime a neighbor came to Tadeusz with news: there are persistent rumors that they are hiding Jews and that "some people" are thinking about reporting this to the police.

After she left the old man brought us the news and told us that we must find another hiding place, temporarily, until the rumors quiet down.

The women break into spasmodic weeping. The men are at a complete loss. To make matters worse, Mrs. F is sick, and Tamara, who has a heart condition, is ill with angina. We decide to send someone over to Antanas to ask whether we can stay with him for a few days. We pack our things and sit down on the bundles to wait for the reply. The fear of death is in everyone's eyes.

When the messenger returns with the information that Antanas cannot take that risk, we grow even more desperate. The last bit of courage that still flickered among us evaporates. Eight Jews sitting on their bundles. Sentenced to death, with no way out. We cannot stay here, and we don't know where else to go.

Observing us in this state must have upset our protectors as well. After a long, oppressive silence, Tadeusz suddenly says: "Children, don't worry. Maybe the devil is not as black as he's painted. Let's wait another few days. Meanwhile, stay here."

One woman could not restrain herself. She ran over and kissed him. The rest of us burst out crying—a release from the tremendous strain of that long, long day. Propped up against the bundles, we try to sleep. May such sleep be granted to all the enemies of the Jews!

DECEMBER 17

The rumors have subsided somewhat, but our fear has not. We are all of the opinion that the wisest thing for us to do would be to move to another place, at least temporarily. But it is precisely in these critical days that the antagonisms among the individuals in our own group become clear. Eight people, each one of us with a different character, a different education, a different approach to fundamental questions. That we are all here together now is only an accident. The differences among us keep us divided.

To the psychological differences have now been added various practical interests: We are looking for ways to save ourselves from death, and those paths are not all leading in the same direction. Some have more money; some are more familiar with the area; others have neither advantage. In the face of death, character differences become sharper. The result is an oppressive tension.

DECEMBER 18

If we are not mistaken, this is the first day of Hanukkah, that bright, childhood holiday. How many happy days it recalls! Even here, in this dark loneliness, we feel the desire (here, even more) to light, one after another, the joyous Hanukkah candles, to part the curtains on the little windows in the cottage and allow the candles to shine on the desolate fields and woods.

An irresistible urge to start singing Hanukkah songs—winged, blissful songs like "*Haneros halolu*" ("These Candles that We Light") and "*Maoz Tsur*" ("Strong Rock of My Salvation"). Oh tiny candles, lit by my father's hand and admired by my mother's eyes—how much we as children sinned against you by taking you for granted and being insensitive to your light and your warmth . . .

DECEMBER 29

Silent, peaceful days—on the surface. Tumultuous, dangerous days beneath.

Because we were unable to sell or barter our possessions, we cannot repay the wealthiest member of our group, the former "plutocrat" (Mr. F), the money he had laid out for food. As a punishment, he ordered his former servant Antanas not to bring us the products he had bought but to store them in his house. For more than a week now we have been living on stale bread and potatoes, and even they will soon be gone. For himself and his wife, he has ordered—and received—meat and fats and is cooking it before our very eyes as we sit there with empty stomachs.

Barbora says to us quietly, but sharply: "Even prisoners in jail share their food with friends."

Tadeusz is more direct. "With the food lying there right under your nose, why should you go hungry?"

On account of money, this former Jewish "plutocrat" grew so agitated today that he got into a terrible row. His shouts could be heard by the neighbors a couple of hundred yards away, which in itself endangered us. But our warnings had no effect on him. Apparently his shouting was part of a well-planned strategy of frightening us in order to make us pay our debt. Waving his fists around, this—what can I call him?—this person screamed at us: "If you don't pay me now my wife and I will leave this place and move to our neighbor's. But whether we do or not, none of you will stay here any longer, not even tonight!"

An open threat to betray us!

And to old Barbora he said: "I'm not afraid of anything! Any Sunday I can get the neighbors together and finish off a bottle with them. And if necessary I can buy off the police too."

This Jew, who had escaped from Hitler but was by no means safe yet, this Jew had not lost his mind. He was speaking these words in full possession of his senses.

Woe to the ears that heard it; woe to those who saw it!

JANUARY 2, 1944

A bite of bread is worth its weight in gold, so we must conserve it, cut it thin, not let a crumb fall to the ground, and most important we must share it in equal portions. When the bread is finished a quarrel begins. This can happen even in a household, let alone among eight strangers. So it is no surprise that today there was a scandal. Raja accused Tamara, who had been working in the kitchen, of giving her own husband more bread than his share. The accused woman responded hysterically: "What! You're watching how much I eat? I'm so weak already that I can hardly stand."

Her husband, Shlomo, joined in: "That's the end! No more! We're not eating anymore! No bread! No potatoes! Nothing!"

A fine state of affairs. A hunger strike in a stable. We plead with them to eat something, but it's no use. Tamara and Shlomo move to one side, whispering to each other. Later that evening, as we're preparing to go into the house, we can't find them. They had both slipped out quietly and are gone. What to do?

Who knows what human beings are capable of in a state of frustration and despair?

We look for them all over. A few hundred yards from the barn we find them hiding in the bushes. After much coaxing we bring them back into the house, but they still refuse to eat anything.

Tadeusz pleads with the husband: "Eat something!"

"No! No!" the husband replies and tries to run out again.

The old man gets angry and grabs Shlomo by the arm. "I've had patience with every one of you, but you don't have any consideration for me? Be a man, not a sheep!" As he says this, Tadeusz raises his hand to hit Shlomo, but we restrain him.

Cannot hunger and the fear of death drive a man out of his mind?

JANUARY 7

The first week of the new year brought us no particular news. Our Jewish plutocrats are still intent on starving us. The potatoes are almost all gone. Six of us look black as earth. The old man can no longer stand our misery, so today, without a word to us, he went over to see Antanas and threatened him with exposure unless he immediately released some of the hidden food to us. This worked. And then this seventy-year-old Lithuanian peasant hoisted a fifty- or sixty-pound sack of food to his shoulder and carried it home through mud and swamp in order to keep six Jews from starving to death.

What is this impoverished Gentile worth compared to our Jewish plutocrat?

JANUARY 10

The severe frosts have begun. Staying in the barn becomes more and more difficult. Most of the day we lie under blankets. It's particularly hard on the feet. Our tight-fitting city shoes are no protection against the cold, and no one had even thought about bringing felt boots.

How shall we hold out the rest of the winter?

JANUARY 15

Tadeusz came home today drunk. His wife berated him. He started beating her unmercifully. We were barely able to rescue her.

These are two doves? Apparently, when arriving at an opinion about someone, you must be very careful, especially in the case of a Lithuanian peasant. "In order to know a person, you have to eat forty pounds of salt with him." The folk know what they're talking about. The Lithuanian peasant is blessed with a primitive cunning he has learned to hide under a mask of innocence.

That's why we were at first misled in our evaluation of the relationship between the old man and his wife. It may be that because of this mask, Jews could not understand the psychology of their Lithuanian neighbors—even after centuries of living together—and therefore their outbreaks of cruelty toward Jews when the Germans invaded the country were for us such a deep, painful puzzle.

Whether this is really the case or not, we now have a new source of trouble. The shattered domestic peace of the old couple has made our own situation here still more precarious.

JANUARY 17

Another argument today between Barbora and Tadeusz. Again he started beating her. It is very disturbing. This time, however, we mind our own business. One cannot always interfere in such matters. Husband-wife conflicts—who knows what the right advice is? It's not justice that determines anything here but blood. Blood and its zig-zag course, with its wild ways and its outbursts.

The old woman had already told us, more than once, that her husband is carrying on with the sister of their neighbor Anulis and that this "other woman" is only waiting for Barbora to die. Whenever Barbora goes away for any length of time (she tells us) the other woman moves into the cottage. Whenever the old man is late coming home in the evening she hisses "Anulis, Anulis . . ." over and over again. Sixty years old and jealous of an eighteen-year-old girl. She lives in constant fear of being betrayed and discarded. Now, in addition, there are beatings and the shame that this is happening in front of us.

She will not tolerate it any longer. "I've had enough! I'm going to stay with the children. They'll be glad to share their poor bread with me."

For us this is a tragedy. Without Barbora we can't stay here another minute longer. So we try to persuade Tadeusz to go easy and make up with her. And we tell her confidentially that by leaving the house now she is putting us all in even greater danger. She takes our advice and stays.

"Only because of you," she tells us. "Without me here, who will take care of you?" We have appealed to the motherly instinct in her, but for how long?

JANUARY 18

We now understand much more clearly the significance of the third plague visited upon the Egyptians. We understand it better because now we are the victims.

Despite all our precautions we are unable to get rid of the lice. Infrequent bathing, sleeping in our clothes for weeks at a time, lying in the hay for hours—all this inevitably brings out the lice. The plague has reached a point where we have lost the shame not only of scratching ourselves but even of actively and openly hunting them out. Like animals do. By day and by night we are in constant battle with our enemy, the lice.

JANUARY 20

A "pleasant anniversary"—three months in the barn.

I am reminded of something that Rabbi Snieg said to me a minute before I left the ghetto, as though he knew where I was going.

There is a verse in Scriptures, he said: "Trust in the Lord; strengthen and encourage your heart, and trust in the Lord." Why does "trust" appear twice? The explanation is: First you are instructed to trust. If this is not enough, then strengthen yourself. If this too is insufficient, then “encourage your heart.” That is, work on yourself still more so that you are able to hope. And if all this is *still* not enough, then again “trust in the Lord.”

The faith of the pious Jew. How true are the words “*ashrey ha-ma'amin*”—happy is the believer. At the worst of times he has someone to whom he can pour out his bitter heart. In the ghetto, before the German actions, and even after the German actions, you could see them, these believers, running with their prayer shawls stuffed under their coats, running to the secret services in order to pour out their hearts to God, to beg, to weep, to ask, to demand. More than once, when I saw them, I felt a pang of envy. More than once I wanted to run to one of those services and murmur a prayer, at least one prayer, as I had done in my childhood, with the same emotional, traditional melody. But somehow I lacked the courage for this.

To crawl under the barbed wire and risk my life—for that I found the courage. To stare into the eyes of death every minute of the day and night—for that I found the courage. But to drop into a service and recite a prayer—for this I could not find the courage. So I exist with a weight on my heart and with tears unshed. How happy is the believer who believes in everything and who justifies everything. How happy is also the apathetic man who has no need of faith at all. He has no questions and he needs no answers. How different it is, however, for the person who is in the middle, who does not believe in God but still occupies himself with godly questions, who thinks about the meaning of his life and the life of his people.

In normal times this is all muddled and muffled by the clamor of living, by one's own personal joys and sorrows. But in bad times—then comes the heavy burden of doubts and disbelief that oppresses the soul. The believer finds a justification for all the acts of the Almighty, even when he doesn't understand them with his common sense: “God and His justice are correct.” But the heart of the nonbeliever is torn apart when his brain finds no answers to the questions that torment him.

The only book I have here with me is a small prayer book. Sometimes I recite one of the prayers, even chant it. But this does not take the weight off my heart. I—and people like me—can recite a prayer, can even chant it, but to ease your heart by means of a prayer, to speak to God through a prayer—that can be done only by a believer.

The various modern movements that gave us so many profound and exalted ideas—they enriched primarily the mind, but they touched the heart less. The emotional world of a believer is richer than the emotional world of a nonbeliever. In life, especially in moments of great personal difficulty, a human being needs not only a crystallized thought but also a crystallized emotion. The modern world is still unable to create for the human being as perfect a way of life as generated by religion. Social ideas, literature, music, dance—all these are not enough to supply a harmonious way of life that will fulfill the "inner soul."

Self-realization through religion for "all" Jews is a problem. Today's Jewish high school is not the traditional cheder, and today's university is certainly not the traditional house of study. The cheder and the house of study were a closed world, and they created a complete way of life with religion. The modern Jewish high school and university are not all-inclusive institutions of religious learning; they are a long way from finding spiritual peace. This may explain why traditionally educated Jewish students live more with their childhood teachings and religious values and why the surroundings of childhood are more deeply etched into their souls than is the case among modern Jewish high school and university students.

With a believer, an "Ecclesiastes mood" always ends with the verse "The end of the matter, all having been heard: Fear God, and keep His commandments; for this is the whole man." Even Job remains with this consolation. (It is not important here whether the theory of the Bible critics is true or not: that this verse was attached later.) An "Ecclesiastes mood" of a nonbeliever, however, hangs on the soul like lead.

Three years in the ghetto and three months in the stable dispose one to think about such matters very often.

JANUARY 27

Today, for the first time, we talked with a stranger. As the dog began barking and we noticed through the cracks that a man with a briefcase under his arm was approaching the cottage, our hearts sank. But it was not as we feared. The stranger turned out to be a peasant carrying a letter from the brother of Moyshe.

From the letter and from the words of the Lithuanian it was clear that the news about the liquidation of the entire ghetto was not correct. Only the first district had been deported. Generally, life in the ghetto is still "normal." New Year's Eve "celebrations" took place there.

The letter also brought us the sad news that Chaim Nachman Shapiro was among those transported out of the ghetto. The American Red Cross had tried to help him by offering him asylum in the United States. Such interventions from abroad always meant death for those being offered asylum.

Dr. Shapiro, son of the rabbi of Kovno and a Hebrew/Yiddish literary critic, was active in Zionist circles in the ghetto. On his initiative a Zionist youth organization was formed there under the name *Eshel*. Considering the circumstances, this group was very active.

Formally (for public consumption and for the government), the goal of *Eshel* was the cultivation of gardens inside the ghetto. Its members even wore a uniform—a pointed white cap. Under this cover they carried out a full program of meetings, lectures on Zionist questions, and singing. Later, the older Zionist youth organizations focused around *Eshel*. Dr. Shapiro was their guiding spirit.

The letter was the first authentic report we saw about the actual situation in the ghetto. The question that had occurred to all of us—"Did we leave the ghetto too soon?"—was answered. Weren't those who argued that there was still time, that we could have waited, now proven wrong?

JANUARY 28

Our plutocrat said to me today, "You fooled me, you know. I thought you had a supply of ten-ruble gold pieces. But now I see that was far from true. I could have made a lot of money out of this hiding place if I had told other Jews in the ghetto."

Keeping my tone as innocent as I could, I asked him: "You're running away from death, and you're still looking for profits?"

Just as calmly he answered me: "As long as you're alive, you have to do business."

Tadeusz thinks I'm an important person. He has noticed that I often sit and write, and this makes a good impression on him. Several times he has awarded me his seal of approval as an educated person. For that reason he often confides in me, as happened today. He tells me that the Jewish plutocrat said to him this morning: "In the ghetto I have a friend who's a doctor. He has a lot of money. If you bring him here you'll get the money, and then you and I can have a party any time we feel like it. They (he meant us) are nothing but a bunch of paupers, beggars, and down-and-outers. Get rid of them!"

Tadeusz commented: "I didn't say a word. I just looked at him, and he could probably read in my eyes what I thought of him."

Our plutocrat is very busy today. In the evening he had another chat with me, but this time he swore me to secrecy. "This place is getting more dangerous for us every day," he told me. The old woman told him that one of her neighbors has been saying openly that she and the old man are hiding Jews. "What do you think we ought to do?" he asked.

His voice is full of fear, and he's clasping and unclasping his hands. I don't trust him. I'm suspicious that he's trying some kind of trickery on us, that he wants to frighten us into leaving this place. Later I ask the old woman if the story he told me is true.

"It's all a lie!" she exclaims. "He did ask me to tell you and the others that story, but I refused to do it."

JANUARY 30

Today our family here grew smaller. The peasant who brought the letter has taken Moyshe home with him. This had been discussed when he was here, but I was the only one who knew about it.

Each of us had contradictory feelings. On the one hand, the fewer the better, because with every passing day it becomes more and more obvious that eight people in one hiding place is too dangerous. On the other hand, there is a gnawing feeling of envy. One person hiding alone is much safer.

FEBRUARY 7

The food that Tadeusz forced Antanas to give us a month ago was all consumed a week ago. Now we don't even have a crust of bread. We are living on watery potato soup, and even that is not available every day in the full amount. The plutocrat and his wife eat their meals right before our eyes—meat and fish and all the trimmings—while we sit and dream about a piece of dry bread. Today he dropped a slice of bread smeared with chicken fat right onto the manure on the ground. All day long I kept my eye on it, and when I remained alone in the stable I grabbed it up and gobbled it down.

I was so ashamed of myself after this "theft" that I could not hold back the tears that came streaming out of my eyes. Were the tears because of the hunger or because of the deterioration of a human being who, for a few hundred marks, can starve his own brothers in a death camp? Who knows the ways of human tears and human joys?

FEBRUARY 10

The extremely cold weather, which had been growing milder, suddenly worsened again. All of us are considerably weaker. Any hope that soon the first warm sunshine will appear has faded. What will we do if the winter turns out to be a long, bitterly cold one?

CHAPTER 4

In The Bushes

FEBRUARY 24

The increasingly severe cold is mitigated by the fact that recently we have not suffered even one setback. This has given us the strength to endure the cold of a Lithuanian countryside while living in a stable. But all the cold weather, and everything else that happened to us in the last four months, are as nothing compared to what happened today.

It was already quite dark when our "commando" group was preparing to slip across the strip of open field between the barn and the house in order to warm up our frozen limbs. But suddenly Tadeusz came running into the barn looking more dead than alive. "Run to the bushes!" he hissed. "Antanas has been arrested! Run!"

A bombshell. So unexpected! We all began to shiver. Some were struck dumb. We wanted to run—but our feet refused to obey. We tried to say something—but our tongues refused to move. Finally someone stammered out a question. But the old man had only one answer: "Run! They'll be here any minute!"

We grabbed whatever we could of our things from the barn—he would not let us into the house—and ran blindly toward the bushes. The old man pointed us to go in a certain direction, but since we've been here we have hardly poked our noses out of our hiding place, so how would we ever find our way in these wild bushes?

But who can stop to ask questions when the Gestapo is only four kilometers away and when we are without doubt the ones they are looking for?

We decided, nevertheless, to take the risk and not get too far away from the house. In the bushes we put down our bundles and prepared to wait. (How much that decision affected our psychological health is hard to say, since we were so close to danger.) What would happen now in the cottage? We assumed that even if the Gestapo did come they would not venture out into the bushes at night, so we had a little time before we needed to start running.

Several hours passed. Nothing happened. We calmed down a bit and then decided to send two people back to the house to pick up our belongings and ask the old woman for at least a loaf of bread.

Frightened to death themselves, our hosts gave us our things in a hurry, because they were also planning to get away from there. When they left they put a lock on the door. Then the old man led his horse deep into the bushes, and he and the old woman hid nearby.

Our plutocrat and his wife were preparing to leave us. Since they know all the peasants in the vicinity, and "money is no object," they are sure they will easily find a new hiding place. Whatever our feelings toward them, at a fateful hour like this we were willing to let bygones be bygones. In the face of death, people often rise above themselves. We said goodbye, we wept, we sobbed. We kissed each other. As the last echoes of their footsteps receded into the silence of the woods, we felt a strange tug at our hearts. For a long time the remaining five of us felt as if we had turned to stone.

We decided to wait there till dawn. Meanwhile we laid our bundles out on the ground and sat down on them. It was so cold we could no longer feel our hands and feet. From time to time we rubbed our hands, ears, and noses with snow to prevent frostbite.

When the first gray dawn came through the bare branches, we got ready to move. To avoid being spotted from a distance, we had to get rid of the most obvious sign of our identity, the knapsacks on our shoulders. We therefore left all our bundles in the bushes along with a marker so we could find them again. We took with us only that which we could absolutely not do without.

None of us will ever forget that death march in the woods. We died of fear a hundred times. Negotiating the endless, serpentine paths was a terrible strain on the nerves for a Jew in the forest, particularly one who has escaped from the ghetto—and now has the Gestapo on his trail! Every rustle, every misstep, the slightest movement of the leaves was a signal of alarm. For us it was a new world.

A strange, wild world. The calls of the birds and the beasts—none of us had ever been in the woods in the middle of the night.

"*Sh-sh!*"

"What?"

Something. A white animal, maybe a forest goat, leaped by us a few yards away, frightening us to death.

Again: "*Sh!* Someone's coming!"

One of us imagined he heard footsteps. We all dropped to the ground and held our breath.

And so on, one shock after another.

How long has this ordeal lasted? We are actually sweating from this "hike" on a Lithuanian winter morning. Our arms are weary from dragging the bundles. At last we find a place in the bushes from which we can see the house of the peasant whom Shlomo and Tamara visited on that unfortunate night of December 9. They deserve a prize for finding their way back from there.

We see but we cannot be seen. We are hidden behind the bushes, and through the branches we watch Shlomo, who is going to negotiate about letting five "passersby" into the barn. When he finally returns and gives us the good news, we are so relieved we all burst out crying. The man has agreed to let us stay, but only for a few days. What more can we expect? Just to rest our bones. For several of us our nerves are stretched so tight that one more turn of the screw could have killed us.

FEBRUARY 25

Again, a new life. We make troughs in the hay of his very large barn. The owners bring us a hot drink and our frozen limbs begin thawing out. After a little nap we try to bring some order into our lives. The peasant has gone off with one of our group to find our hidden bundles—all our worldly goods, the only things we own that we can exchange for food.

The short February day passes quickly. Evening comes, and our mood improves. Hope returns. Perhaps they will let us stay here. Suddenly the peasant runs in, all out of breath: "They are searching the whole neighborhood, every house! I'm afraid! Get out! Now!"

After a moment of oppressive silence, he adds: "I fell asleep before and had a terrible dream. Seven priests dressed in black, with big black crucifixes on their chests, are walking toward me, pointing their fingers. A bad omen; Jesus have mercy! I read it myself in the book of dreams—it's a sign of terrible misfortune. Can't you hear it? Dogs barking. Strangers approaching my neighbor's house. Police."

Frightened, we plead with him. "Let us stay here at least for tonight." The women weep; they kiss his hand.

He agrees, but on one condition: at daybreak, we leave. Thus our new hope quickly dissolves. Again we are left without a way out. Again we face a dark abyss.

FEBRUARY 26

A new day, new troubles.

With the first light of morning we gather up all our bundles. We toss them over our shoulders and practically crawl across the yard between the barn and the bushes. It's still very early, but there is no darkness to protect us, and here in these strange bushes we must find a way to conceal ourselves and wait for the arrival of dusk so that we can again be on our way.

Exhausted, without sleep, without food, without a spark of hope and without a plan—or anything resembling a plan—in our heads, we sit down on our bundles among the snow-covered bushes. Suddenly my wife loses her balance, grabs hold of me, and whispers, "I feel sick!" Her eyes have a peculiar, unnatural look. Disquieting thoughts about her mental condition flash through my mind. Her sister, Nechama, puts us all in danger by running into the peasant's home for an egg and a bottle of milk. The food brings about a change in my wife. Her eyes slowly regain their normal look, and after a couple of disturbing hours she is again in control of herself.

From our new hosts we had managed to learn, by asking them subtle questions, that the Gestapo has not been at Tadeusz's house or anywhere else in the neighborhood during the last twenty-four hours. We asked indirectly because they are not supposed to know where we have been hiding! Having no other choice, we decide to walk toward our former hiding place. As soon as darkness falls, our whole column sets out, and without incident and without getting lost we make it back. As we approach "our" bushes, we are enveloped by a warm feeling of familiarity. Home!

How comforting that one simple word sounds now! The broken-down cottage, the barn, the horse, Tadeusz and Barbora, the dog—it has all grown so familiar to us that our heavy hearts grow a little lighter.

But suddenly—footsteps!

Again a deadly fear overwhelms us. We look at each other mutely. We listen, we try to make ourselves smaller, invisible.

The footsteps grow louder. Our nerves are at a breaking point. There is nothing we can do but remain motionless.

A creature leaps at us—our dog!

He embraces us with such elation that we can see it in his eyes. He brushes up against each of us, licks us, runs away a few feet, lopes back, rolls in the snow, and does all his tricks. Crazy!

We are moved to tears. The only living creature in the world that is not hunting us, that is not afraid of us, that is genuinely happy to see us. Bless you, dear little dog, for your loyalty, for the comfort you bring us, the wretched and the hunted!

Following the dog's tracks, the old couple also find us. They have come to tell us that the Gestapo has not yet visited them. They feel more optimistic now, and they try to cheer us up. Barbora brings a pot of hot cabbage soup, the best soup I ever tasted.

Shall we ever be able to repay this debt, or will it remain, God forbid, an unreciprocated good deed?

Hearing from our hosts that they are planning to leave their cottage that same night and stay away for several weeks, Tamara and Shlomo decide that they will separate from us and try their luck in another direction. So there are only three of us left—my wife, her sister, and myself.

Our spirits plummet. My wife starts to have hallucinations. She grabs my hand and whispers:

"Those bushes—they're moving! The trees—they are living corpses! I'm scared to death! Over there—there's a man! I can see his face! We've got to run! I'm afraid! Let's run away from here!"

The cold is unbearable. We must do something at once or we will all freeze to death. We decide to crawl on all fours toward the cottage. When we get there, we see that the old couple have kept their word. There's a lock on the door.

We slip into the barn. The horse is not there, a sure sign that our protectors have gone away. They must really have expected a visit from the Gestapo. But we have no choice. We collapse on the hay and fall asleep, only to be assailed by one nightmare after another, all with the same theme: Gestapo, Gestapo, Gestapo.

We took a big risk staying there all night, and once more we retreat to the bushes in the morning.

FEBRUARY 27

The first "normal" day in the bushes. We decide to make this our permanent "home." We choose a thicket, find a tall pine tree that offers more protection because of its dense needles, and lie down on our bundles. We do not speak, and we are sparing of our bodily movements.

Every bark of the dog echoing through the trees causes us to shudder. Previously, the barking was a signal that a stranger was in the vicinity. Now it's the Gestapo. The longer the barking lasts, the higher the tension mounts.

When it ceases, we take a deep breath, as people do in a beleaguered city when the bombardments stop.

The final days of February have brought even worse frosts. The sun is shining, but it brings us no warmth. Our feet are especially vulnerable. The women cover their feet with rags and coats and sit in one place for hours.

The days pass without incident, and before darkness falls we move closer to the cottage, making as little noise as possible. This is not easy. Because of the frost every footstep creaks, and the branches that we must push aside with our hands crackle so loudly that it seems they will be heard for miles around. But there is no help for it because there are no footpaths to follow.

The bushes are a new world for us, with their stunted trees, their birds and animals. They are a labyrinth, and we get lost in them. Take five steps and you have trouble finding your way back.

When we finally crawl across the open field and, like thieves in the night, sneak over to the door, the lock is still in place, and we again slip into the barn for a night's lodging.

FEBRUARY 28

A joyous occasion. The old man has come back for us in the bushes and brought us hot food. He invites us to come to the house tonight to warm our frozen bones. Not often in life does an invitation bring such immeasurable happiness!

The old woman gives us more details about the upsetting events of February 24. The post office in Vilkija was holding a letter addressed to "Berelis Kaganas" c/o Antanas. The letter was immediately forwarded to the Gestapo in Kovno, and they were the ones who raided the house.

We stare at each other in consternation. Who could have sent such a letter? A friend from the ghetto? Informers? But how could that be, when we ourselves did not know Antanas's address?

A great puzzle that we have not been able to solve. The old woman also tells us that the first day after Antanas's arrest, Tadeusz was grief-stricken. He was so depressed that he lost his senses and tried to hang himself in the bushes. She barely got to him in time.

How delicious the warmth of the house is now. One's limbs seem to melt, and relaxation and warmth bring sleep quickly.

A loud barking awakens us. Then comes a knock at the door. Who? Tamara and Shlomo have come back. No one out there wants to take them in. People are ready to let them spend the night, and even to feed them, but no one lets them stay any longer than that. So our family has increased again, but this time not so happily because resources are limited.

MARCH 1

Today we suddenly realize that in running from death, we forgot about something that meant life: the chunk of meat that we left hanging in the attic. We looked, we searched, but we could not find it anywhere. Suspicions and accusations flew, but to no avail. A piece of meat in our situation is a piece of life, so we can't simply overlook it. We continue to investigate until it finally emerges that the meat "fell" into a sack belonging to one of our company. In the confusion and panic, with the Gestapo on our necks, when ten or fifteen minutes meant the difference between life and death, one of our number did not lose his nerve. Unnoticed, he climbed up to the attic and took the meat, which belonged to all of us, for himself.

Now it turns out that something else has disappeared: my razor and all my blades with it. What shall I do now? Seemingly trivial things in our situation could mean danger. By not shaving, my "Jewish appearance" will be more easily recognized—it will be a new source of danger.

Naturally I am angry, but I am also curious. What kind of person, whose life is hanging by a thread, can even think about such things as meat and razors? The answer: precisely the kind of person who has more chance of surviving than the rest of us.

In the ghetto, who has survived up to now? Those who never lose their presence of mind, even in the face of extreme danger, and those who have faith. Actually, they are one and the same. The person who has faith is the one who doesn't lose his presence of mind. The person who went to an "action" with a chunk of bread in his pocket held out the longest. Those who gave up in despair did not even think about bread. Of what use is bread to a dead man? And if it happened that death was temporarily postponed, those who were resigned to die had nothing with which to keep body and soul together.

In the ghetto, miracles happen only to those who believe in them. And the same will hold true here in the bushes.

MARCH 2

Today there are five of us. The women sit with their feet wrapped in rags. We count the hours of the day and we yearn for the night.

Human beings? Bats!

Now we are again sitting by the oven, happy that we survived another day. Suddenly a knock at the window breaks into our reverie. A prearranged signal. The two "plutocrats" (Mr. and Mrs. F) are back. It is difficult to recognize them, they have changed so drastically in only a few days. Dirty, crushed. He is unshaven. No longer the snob, no longer giving himself airs, no longer full of spirit. The family has once again grown. It is obvious that our hosts are not happy. After they have become accustomed to protecting only three Jews, they wouldn't want seven. What shall we do? We go to sleep thinking we will have to wait until tomorrow.

Today there are five of us. The women sit with their feet wrapped in rags. We count the hours of the day and we yearn for the night.

MARCH 3

Seven of us hiding together in the bushes is quite complicated. There is too much movement, especially when a person like our plutocrat is one of the seven. During the night he sobered up and became his old self again, creating tumult. Money, gold, you owe me. He cannot rest if he thinks that someone else has a piece of gold and is keeping it for an emergency. Here is a man sentenced to death by Hitler—and all he can think of is that someone owes him a couple of hundred marks.

"If you don't have the money to pay the debt, give me your coat as security!" He screams, makes a scene, wants to fight. The rest of us are outraged. Here in the bushes, he's carrying on like this, where every whisper reverberates and where the least sound can kill us all.

What shall we do? Choke one Jewish money lender to death to save six other Jews? Or give in to him? Suddenly my wife pulls off a new woolen dress (which she is wearing over another one) and throws it in his face—in the freezing cold in the middle of the woods!

On account of one person like this a whole city can be destroyed. On account of two like this, a whole people can be destroyed.

MARCH 4

Immediately after this incident the plutocrats left again. That same day Tamara and Shlomo left too. So now we are three poor souls again. Our daily routine: during the day, in the bushes; at night, in the barn. But now we have a new problem. We have finished our last bit of bread. This is our third day of fasting. Because our landlords have been away for a few days we do not even have any water.

Desperate, we decide to take a very dangerous step. My wife's sister, who does not look typically Jewish and who speaks Lithuanian like a native, will go out and exchange some of our belongings for food. We hope she can get enough food to last a few weeks.

It's not difficult to imagine our state of mind as we send out our messenger. But the mission proves successful—even beyond our expectations. That evening, like locusts, we attack the bread, the ham, and the bottle of sweet cream. On our way to the barn, however, we hear footsteps behind us and stop in our tracks. Then a voice says in Lithuanian: "Friends, where are you running to?"

In the bushes you can't see another person when he is at a distance. This man sprang out of the earth not ten meters behind us. It was useless to run. We turn around, and before us is an ordinary peasant. Is this meeting accidental, or had he been following us? Smiling, he tells us he could recognize immediately who we were. We try to make the best of it. "We are in a Jewish work brigade. The Germans allowed us to go and exchange some things for money."

He bids us a hearty farewell, comforts us with the hope that things will soon be better, and goes on his way. Did he really mean that, or was it the blessing of a spy?

MARCH 12

The extraordinary meeting in the bushes left us shaken. But when no suspicious signs appeared for several days, we relaxed and forgot it.

For a while the days were quiet and without incident. In a diary like this, those words must seem peculiar. But aside from the usual unusual experiences, nothing special happened. The tinkling of cowbells early and late. The shouts of the shepherds. The love song of a village shepherdess. The constant chirping of the birds. The barking of dogs.

That was all.

MARCH 16

It is the middle of March, yet the bitter cold days hang on. Just our luck! We have little food. Every day we wish our plight on Hitler! But there's no help for it. Day in, day out, we stand in the bushes, frozen blue, and count the hours. A new kind of Omer. We talk a little, in whispers, so that the wind does not carry the sound to the wrong ears. We sink into fantasies of a bright future. In our thoughts we bring the end closer, and that helps us go on living. If that becomes tedious, we unfold the German or Lithuanian newspapers that we picked up weeks ago. We speculate about the changes that might have taken place since then. Everything to our advantage, naturally, because the embittered and tortured heart must find a little elixir of life to sustain it.

In a situation of deadly peril, one performs a wide variety of tricks that enable you to run away from death, at least in your mind. In your imagination you construct a new world for yourself. For a little while you forget about death, standing in the rain and snow in the Lithuanian bushes, fearful of every movement in the woods.

This prescription does not work for very long. They quickly dissolve, those artificially created fairy lands, and in their place the Angel of Death appears a hundred times a day and sucks out the little bit of marrow that is left in your bones.

Every rustle, every crackle of a twig, every bark of a dog, every sound of a passing wagon—everything gives birth to a thought: They're after me. They will catch me. They are leading me—to death.

Death. Today we experienced it even more sharply. We are sitting there deep in our own thoughts, everyone in his own world, when we hear footsteps. We could recognize the footsteps of old Barbora, but these are not hers. We shrivel up. Our hearts are beating like clocks. Our limbs tremble. The footsteps keep getting louder. Out of the bushes comes a figure, a man in a leather jacket. We hold our breath. One turn in our direction and he must see us. But then the miracle happens. He does not turn his face toward us. And gradually he disappears among the bushes.

Death and death and death, from every direction. How does one escape it?

MARCH 18

Our two plutocrats, Mr. and Mrs. F, show up once more. No one is letting them stay long in any one place; having old acquaintances doesn't help any more. The peasants in the area are becoming more and more intimidated. The old man lets them stay, but his heart isn't in it.

Our not-too-welcome guests bring us a "wonderful" piece of news: Antanas, who provided us with bread, and whose arrest on February 24 forced us to flee to the bushes, is about to be freed. As a result, we are all worried sick about one thing: Will he betray us? We know very well the methods by which the Gestapo persuades people to talk.

Tadeusz has told us more than once what he heard from Antanas's wife, that the Gestapo said to Antanas: "Just tell us where those Jews are hiding and we'll let you go free immediately."

They tortured him with their whole assortment of instruments, but he did not betray this handful of Jews.

Antanas—one of the Gentile friends of Jews.

MARCH 18

Today our hosts rode into the city once more, leaving us the key to their cottage. We decided to enter the house later than usual, because if anyone were to visit that evening, they must find no one home. But as if to spite us, the pig breaks out of his stall, and we have to chase after him. We finally catch him, but as we are taking him back to the barn I suddenly notice the silhouette of a person about ten meters away.

I start to retreat, but Raja, who has the pig in her arms, goes straight into the barn, and I have no choice but to follow her. Inside the barn we divide into three groups and do not communicate with each other. For three hours we keep apart without even a whisper. Then, after the signal of a cough from the pig stall, we slip into the cottage in complete silence. Even there we do not utter a word or light any candles.

Who could that person have been? A thief? A spy? A passerby? If it was a complete stranger, why had he not asked for food, or directions, or whatever? Perhaps he even went into the barn. This thought distressed us so much we were afraid we would go out of our minds. If we had acted logically, we would have run away from there at once. But where to? Once again we placed ourselves in the hands of blind fate, and like shipwrecked sailors hanging on to pieces of wreckage, we let ourselves be carried on the waves, hoping that eventually we would drift ashore.

MARCH 19

We have been maligning the frosts. With them we could at least sit down on the fallen tree trunks and wrap our feet in rags. Now that the snow is melting and the swamps are everywhere, we trudge through water and mud in our city shoes and we are soaked through to the skin. At night we hang our clothes and shoes over the oven so that the next day we can get them wet again. For three weeks we have not washed. The lice are busy, and we are busy scratching shamelessly, using not only our fingers but even splinters of pine.

Whoever has not experienced this torture cannot even imagine what a plague this is. We are literally covered with lice. It is not just a figure of speech that they suck the blood out of you. You cannot stand still for a second. You must jump around. They congregate especially in all the places in your clothing that have holes or creases, in your socks and in the seat of your trousers. The solution would be to throw away our clothes and put on new ones. Where would we get them? Or we could soak them in boiling water. But could we stand in the bushes or the stable naked while the clothes dry?

How much longer can we endure this plague?

MARCH 20

Dawn. We gulp down a pot of hot tea and go back into the bushes. But God Almighty, what weather this is! Snow and the wind howling in gusts. It takes every ounce of strength to stay upright. How can we possibly survive in the bushes on a day like this? The old man, who lets us out the door, seems to read our thoughts and lets us take only a few steps away from the house before running after us, shouting: "Oh to the devil with it all! Stay in the stable today!" We had not expected this. The women weep for joy. The stable looks like a palace to us now. After weeks in the snow-covered bushes, this place seems homey and comfortable to us—the horse, the hay, the crumbling walls.

How warm it is here! We stretch out on the hay, as if it were a bed in a hotel. Our situation reminds me of a deeply psychological story about a goat the rabbi advised to take into a house.

MARCH 26

A few restful days, but then terrible news. Peasants tell us that the Germans have taken all the children out of the ghetto. One mother killed a Lithuanian policeman with an axe as he was trying to take her child from her. She was shot on the spot.

Is it possible that those precious, lovely little swallows in the ghetto are being dragged to the deep dark pits? I ask myself that question even though I know how foolish it sounds.

Along with this dreadful news, we get hold of a newspaper today that reports major Soviet breakthroughs on the southern front, as well as at Leningrad and Pskov, which for us is even more important.

Will the ghetto live to see the hour of deliverance?

APRIL 4

Even during the worst troubles, time does not stand still. The days, though heavy as lead, still move, and the nights, with their horrible nightmares, also move in their infinite course. Already it is early April. Our food situation keeps growing worse.

Sometimes we get some potato soup, sometimes not even that. The same with bread. There are signs of physical deterioration in everyone. Some of us are beginning to have severe headaches and dizziness.

Our horse is now on a "diet," so the old man brings some turnips for him. When the old man leaves, we attack the trough and steal a couple of turnips from the horse's portion. We scraped them with a knife and enjoyed them immensely.

Hunger!

Ever since the last big storm, we've been living in the stable every day. Today, for the first time, a real spring sun shines into our living quarters. We all run from the damp hay to the cracks in the wall, through which come the first, bright refreshing rays.

Through the cracks we can see a narrow strip of the outdoors.

How beautiful God's little world is!

And we?

According to our calculations this should be the first day of Passover. Who can better understand and experience the exodus from Egypt than an escaped ghetto Jew hiding in a stable? I am reminded of the brilliant words in the Haggadah: "As the Lord our God delivered us from Egypt, so He will deliver us from slavery to freedom, from subjugation to liberation, from darkness to great light."

When, dear Father in Heaven? When?

APRIL 8

Very soon we will run out of potatoes. The bread is all gone. Again, we decide on the riskiest step: to go out into the nearby villages and exchange some of our belongings for food. It is clear this course is dangerous not only for the one who goes out but for the entire group. But we are at the end of our tether.

That night none of us could sleep. We were busy with preparations, getting our "wares" ready—handkerchiefs, dresses, pieces of goods. With the moon still out, Nechama starts out on her perilous journey, with her good Lithuanian speech, her peasant garb, and the pack of merchandise in a farmer's basket.

All day long our thoughts are with her. Twilight comes and our anxiety mounts. According to our plan, she should have been back before nightfall. We do not move from the barn at our usual time. Nothing else is on our minds except her return.

When we finally hear her footsteps, a heavy weight falls from our hearts. There is a double celebration: for the end of the danger and for the bundle she has brought back.

APRIL 10

Tadeusz returns from the village with some more bad news. In one house in the area, Lithuanian partisans found three Jews in hiding. They shot the Jews on the spot and hanged the members of the household. In a neighboring town they led two Jews through the streets; they had caught them in the home of a peasant. People are warning each other not to hide Jews in their homes because if they are caught even the neighbors are punished. In one house Tadeusz was told plainly that there are rumors he is hiding Jews.

These stories affected us greatly. Recently we had noticed a marked change in the old man, although we had no clear idea what it meant. We have a feeling—so far it's only an intuition—that he has changed fundamentally. From his small, narrow eyes there comes a dark look. We suspect he is wrestling with his conscience: to do it or not to do it.

A few days ago he said to Nechama, "What shall I do? Drive you out? I don't have the heart for that. Turn you over to the police? I can't do that either. I feel sorry for you. But my life is precious to me too."

What has happened to the old man upon whom our very lives depend? Can this generous protector of ours allow the thought into his mind to betray us? Is he walking around with murderous thoughts in his head? We try to find an explanation that will exonerate him, but the words he uttered cannot be dismissed. It frightens us and nags at us and won't let up.

What has really happened to him all of a sudden? Has he grown weary of us? We are aware that he has been putting up with us for almost six months, and it's no wonder that he wants to be rid of the constant fear of being caught by the Gestapo. But we are only flesh and blood; we want to live, too, and not have to worry about every little thing.

I recall how in the first months he used to maintain that he had no fear of death, that he had lived a full life and now he wants to save a few innocent souls. And now? Has the approach of danger decreased his bravery and dulled his idealism? Has the test gone on too long to be endured?

Or is it because with each passing day it has become more and more difficult to find food, and our means of support is on the verge of drying up altogether? True, he is not a bloodsucker, and we have come to appreciate that. But after all, poverty is neither a disgrace nor an honor. Nor does it inspire love, the kind of love for which you risk your own life. Still, something has happened to him. What is it?

We cannot penetrate the depths of his soul, but we have grown accustomed to living one day at a time and rejoicing when the day is over.

God blesses us from day to day.

APRIL 13

A sunny day. Spring is in the air. We crawl out of our beds. Bright light streams through the cracks, bringing a bit of joy and comfort.

Spring. When will our spring come?

That our lives are still wintry is proven later that same day. As soon as darkness falls two of us slip into the house, and the others prepare to do the same. Suddenly the dog is barking. At the door of the house is a man with a whip, and he quickly runs into the house. Did the first two have time to hide?

After the person leaves the two come running into the barn. "We've got to go back to the bushes!" One of them is paralyzed with fear. The other one loses her power of speech. We can barely understand what she is saying and try to calm her down.

Finally they tell what happened. They managed to hide inside the house by climbing up onto the oven and covering themselves up. From there they were able to hear the peasant with the whip warn our old couple that in a house nearby a violent Lithuanian partisan is spending his leave. The neighbor had heard him say that he is coming to inspect Tadeusz's house because he had heard that Jews are hiding there. Barbora had jumped up from her chair, moaning, "Oh Jesus! Oh Jesus!"

The neighbor ended with the comment that it could happen "tonight or tomorrow morning." He begged them not to say anything about his warning, because it could cost him his life.

Again we pack up our things and tie up our bundles. Barbora takes us to the bushes. Mud. Swamps. Often it seems that we won't be able to pull our feet out. In the darkness we can barely see where to walk among these wild bushes. The branches scratch our hands and faces. It must have been around midnight when we heard the old man's hoarse whisper: "When things quiet down, you can come back. We've kept you safe up to now. We'll keep on doing so. We'll bring you food. In the morning, move deeper into the bushes."

We are trying to figure out what has happened. This time all the excitement has something staged about it. We have serious doubts. The old people have told us that the bearer of the latest news was our close neighbor Anulis. But Anulis is a short man, middle aged, and he has only one arm. As far as we could tell in the twilight, looking through the cracks, the visitor was a man with both arms, and in any case he was much taller than Anulis. Furthermore, if it really was Anulis, then why, at the same moment he was here, was Tadeusz visiting him? During the visit Tadeusz was not at home, and the old woman told us that her husband had gone to visit Anulis. The words of the neighbor were also peculiar. They sounded like a memorized speech. Tadeusz's current behavior was also very suspicious. During the excitement in February he was scared to death and allowed no one else to say a word. This time he stayed calm and sat quietly on the bed while the old woman described the man who had come to see him.

Our painful doubts are interrupted by the swishing of branches. A few moments later we hear what sounds like growling. In the moonlight we can see, not ten steps away from us, an enormous hog, probably a wild one. Is it in the habit of attacking humans, we wonder? We pick up thick branches from the ground and wait.

The forest animal shrinks back, however, apparently frightened off by the weapons of the strong men of Israel.

Miracles. Miracles. Miracles.

CHAPTER 5

A Jew In The Forest

APRIL 14

In the morning, half asleep and exhausted, we again put our bundles on our shoulders. We slog through swamps, often up to our knees, until we find a new place that, according to our calculations, was deep in the bushes, well concealed, and far away from roads and even footpaths. We have not yet had time to admire our new home when the old woman comes running up, all excited: "God in heaven! Why did you ever pick this spot? You are too close to the main road!"

Shaken, we again put our belongings on our shoulders and follow the old woman. Her words are alarming. "This is too close to the house. The old man will come out later and take you to a place a few kilometers from here where there is a big forest that stretches for miles."

This is completely unexpected. Our suspicions are again aroused. They want to get rid of us . . .

The old man comes and we follow him. We leave a distance of about twenty steps between each person. Several times we cut across the highway, which is most dangerous, but we have no choice. It is still early in the morning. Nothing is moving yet on the roads. More mud, more swamp. The women tire and cannot go on. We stop and rest.

It is late morning by this time, and Tadeusz says that we still have far to go to reach the place he had in mind for us. We are to stay here, he says, and at dusk he will come back and lead us to our new place of refuge.

Another hike, the fifth in one day.

We had already become accustomed to the bushes, but the forest, with its tall trees, is a new experience for us. When we arrive at the appointed place, we immediately look for a spot where the trees are closer together as protection against rain and accidental passersby. Night falls and we quickly prepare our beds. We pull up some grass for a mattress that might give us some protection against the damp earth, and we prepare long thick branches to use against the wild animals that are plentiful here.

That first night we hardly shut our eyes. Animals of all sorts scream and growl. Every other minute we reach for our weapons, but apparently the local forest creatures are afraid of humans. As soon as they get the scent of one they flee. Obviously, they do not understand Hitler's "race theory." They count a few bone-weary Jews among the race of human beings.

APRIL 15

The twittering of the birds awakens us from our few hours of dozing and, contrary to our usual luck, the sun welcomes us in a most friendly manner. Our inner turmoil, brought on by the events of two nights ago, gradually dies down to be replaced by a certain calm; perhaps, after all, we will be safer here than we were in the cottage.

The freshness of the air is almost palpable. We fill our lungs with it. Our pale cheeks reflect the rays of the sun. Like travelers in the desert, we throw ourselves upon the little stream that we stumble on. We sprinkle our hair and open our shirts. Water! Water! Refreshed and cleansed, we stand on little mounds or on the branches of trees and warm ourselves in the sun, sighing ecstatically.

When did we ever so fully appreciate the power of the sun? When did we ever bless it so feelingly, not only with our mouths but with our whole bodies? In these conditions, it becomes crystal clear why thousands of years ago people thought of the sun as a god and bowed and prayed to it. In the twentieth century we too pray to it in the forest. Where are the words to describe the feelings that, at the first rays of the sun, surge up in the souls of those who have escaped from death, or even from a stable?

For a few moments we forget our troubles. Who else besides a Jew grows accustomed so easily to misfortune? "You know, it's not so bad here so long as nobody walks in on us," someone says. In the ghetto and in the barn I learned to keep quiet while someone else was saying things that expressed hope and faith in deliverance, even though I didn't believe it. To express doubts, except in a moment of real danger, means to commit spiritual theft.

The women even take out our scant bedclothes and spread them out in the sun on a bit of open field near our shelter. We hang our other clothing on the branches, and sometimes it almost feels as if we are here on vacation. One person felt so safe here that he proposed that we light a fire and make ourselves some tea! One thing we do not have to be careful of here is our voices. We no longer have to speak in whispers. This place is like an island. We drink the fresh air into our dusty lungs, sit in the sun, and talk our heads off, all the while smiling (against our own will) at the good move we have made.

"*Am Olam*." Eternal People. The secret and the cause of this lies perhaps in the fact that Jews can appreciate the moment. From that comes their extraordinary ability to adapt to the most inhuman conditions. Lithuanians have already said to us more than once, "We could never stand it. We would have hit somebody with an axe—it is your life or mine. But to live as you are now living, that we could never do." Most likely this feeling is greatly exaggerated, because we haven't seen any big revolutions started by non-Jews against the Germans, but there is an element of truth in those words.

The psychological and spiritual elasticity of Jews is one of the great miracles of Jewish survival. In miniature, it is even evident in our own little settlement here. We live for the day, with today's shining sun, with today's refreshing air, and we store up energy and strength for the better days that are sure to come.

The warm air makes us thirsty. We go to our stream, draw some water, show it to the women for their opinion. The color is yellowish. The water has a bad taste and something else besides: tiny black bugs. The dark yellow water in the blue pot is reminiscent of something unpleasant, and that does not make it any easier to drink.

But thirst is even stronger than hunger. The first few sips are difficult, but after that it's not so bad. Has the water lost its taste, or have we? What is the difference, so long as it's water. What would we have done if we had found no water here at all? We say "*gam zu l'tova*"—this too is for the best—and that takes care of all objections.

I am reminded of something the Lithuanian mayor of my hometown, Telšiai, used to say: "When a Christian breaks his leg he screams bloody murder and complains, 'Oh Jesus!' But it's no consolation. When something like that happens to a Jew he screams just as loud, but he soon finds solace: 'Thank God I didn't break both legs!'"

APRIL 16

We are not fated to have a moment's rest. It appears that Tadeusz made a bad mistake when he chose this spot, because nearby there is a major road. Yesterday it could have all been up for us. A good thing for us that "God watches over fools." But this time Tadeusz has thoroughly checked out another new spot. He assures us that only by sheer accident would anyone stumble over us there.

The new place is protected by tall dense trees and a few smaller ones. Anyone passing by here would have to look hard to notice it. Even so we still decide to camouflage our living quarters. First, we need to put up a few walls. For this purpose we use the smaller pine trees, which grow plentifully here. We have no axe, so we pull them up by the roots. This is not easy to do, so two of us hitch ourselves together.

We try this only where the ground is a little damp or soft. In the dry places we are no match for the large roots. We then replant these trees around our "house" and inside we pile up the grass. This makes us feel a little safer. Of course, the sky is still our roof, but we must protect ourselves against the creatures on the ground, not those in the sky.

The day passes quickly. We are so busy with our building project that before we realize, darkness has fallen. Only the highest treetops are still enjoying the last rays of the setting sun. We arrange our beds, we talk a while, we chew our dry bread, and finally we pull our coats over our faces and say good night!

A Jewish child in the forest! Was there ever a greater incongruity? When a Jewish child used to do something naughty in the old, now forever-gone shtetl, he would be threatened with "Gypsies in the forest." "Forest" was a scare word not only for little Moisheles and Shloymeles but also for grown-ups. Riding through a forest at night on a horse and wagon meant taking your life in your hands. People prepared for such journeys in groups, and more than one passenger stayed home if he could not find a carriage that had other passengers in it.

And the ride itself—women would keep their eyes shut tight, men would recite chapters from Psalms, and the drivers would give themselves courage by keeping a wooden club at their side. The forest was a place for thieves and robbers, a world far removed from Jews and the Jewish way of life. More than one of us here now, even if you had offered him thousands of rubles, would not have had the nerve to go into the forest alone at night.

Almost every story that the Jewish child hears about ghosts and evil spirits has to do with the forest. A calf, all tied up in a wagon, disappears in the middle of the forest, crowing like a rooster. A flame winks in the distance during a forest journey on a dark, rainy night—winks and lures weary travelers to their deaths. In every Lithuanian town there were Jews who were known for having suffered during one of these journeys. And it would all be repeated in the conversations between afternoon and evening services in the synagogue, especially as the Sabbath ended and wide-eyed Jewish children would soak all this up into their fluttering hearts. Thus, over the years, the forest was transformed by the imagination into a symbol of everything evil. The forest threatens and terrorizes, and now—now we live in the forest, now we sleep in the forest, now the forest is our protector.

APRIL 17

Today again we work all day building our bunker. We work with the zeal of ants, and we accomplish more and more. Rarely has a house had such a responsibility as ours for life and death. One crack through which a mean-spirited eye could look and the whole game would be up.

For a little while our work is interrupted by old Tadeusz. He tells us that lately he has had a number of visitors, and he suspects that not all of them had innocent intentions. Especially suspicious were two young fellows who had no questions to ask him except about his opinions on the war and on Jews. He also tells us that the dog barks all night long. Apparently someone is watching the house, trying to catch him red-handed. He can't sleep at night. He is so scared. He paces around the house, afraid to go out.

Our brave Tadeusz. See what can happen to a man!

Apparently it is very hard for people to overcome their weaknesses, even in dangerous situations. No matter how often we have been warned, we simply cannot spend all our time inside the bunker. It is, by the way, cool inside our shelter, and the temptation to go out and warm up in the sun is irresistible. We also do not always observe the rule that only one of us at a time should uproot the shrubs, so that if a stranger happens along, it would be easier to get out of sight. Instead, we all go out together, and sometimes it happens that with our nerves stretched so tight, someone imagines he hears an unfamiliar sound and rushes to the shelter, which starts a panicky dash inside. We must look like soldiers diving into a ditch during an air attack. In reality what has happened is nothing except a hallucination. Oh, the nerves, the nerves—how they sap us of our last bit of strength.

APRIL 18

If we live to get out of these hundred hells, we will have a new occupation—astronomy. We never stop looking up at the heavens. In the first place, we all love the sight of the blue sky. In the second place, we need to determine the time by the sun, because none of us has a watch. A peculiar thing. In the days when we were all working and had watches, we did not look at them so often. Here, however, in our idleness, we are continually asking, "I wonder what time it is now?" as though the other person was in a better position to know. How quickly adults are transformed into young children!

In the third place, we keep studying the sky to see if it is growing darker, God forbid. The thing we are most afraid of is that the sky will start pouring down water upon us.

Astronomers! In our shtetl we knew very little about that science. We called them simply "sky watchers." In every town there were people whom the locals crowned with that title. Usually they were poetically inclined people who looked at the sky more than they did the earth, or else they were simply people who, because of the way they walked, kept their eyes turned more to The One Above.

Joking aside, our own particular piece of sky was beginning to take on an unpleasant appearance. Very often the sun would disappear and dark clouds would chase each other across the sky. Mrs. F has a touch of rheumatism. She already has cramps in her leg—a sure sign that the weather is about to change. We are getting ready to turn in, and the cloudy sky and our human barometers are not helping us feel good at all.

Later that evening the old woman comes with several small bread loaves, which are supposed to last all week because they don't have enough bread themselves, and no one knows when a new delivery will arrive.

APRIL 19

I had not yet fallen asleep when I heard someone saying: "Well, what do you say to this rain, huh?"

What is there to say when the rain is dripping on your head and we must gather everything up, including the bedclothes? And how are you going to pack up when it's black as coal and you can't see your own hand in front of your face? We throw our things blindly into the sacks, cover them with twigs and whatever else we can pick up, and rush out to seek shelter under the branches of the tall, thick pines.

"Rush out" is only an expression. It's so dark you're afraid to take a single step. We hold each other's hands and step along stiffly like blind people toward the tree. But where is it? All we can see is a mass of fused blackness. Up above, the darkness relents a little and you can see the tops of the highest trees. The tree toward which we are heading seemed only a few steps away, but when we reach it, it isn't there. Instead, we collide with shrubs that scratch our hands and faces. Now we know why so many magical legends have to do with nighttime in the forest.

We try to go forward. What is this? Our hearts hammer in alarm. A few yards away we see a pair of eyes gleaming in the darkness. After a moment of panic I reach into my pocket for the weapon I have known about all my life: a match, fire. But what if it's not a wolf but a snake?

"What should we do?" I ask my wife, who is holding on to my arm and shivering with fear and cold. Instinctively we change direction and run away from those horrible eyes. The next morning we learn the explanation for those wolfish eyes: rotting moss, which contains phosphorous!

Even the dense trees give us no protection from this downpour. Our clothes are soaked through. We shiver in the cold. To spite us, the forest animals are also wide awake. A wild goat bleats mournfully. A hog grunts. Some other kinds of animals that we haven't met yet make their unnatural noises. Our introduction to night in the forest is endless. We keep looking up at the sky. The pale streaks up there are growing brighter and reflections appear down below. The blackness gradually dissolves into gray.

We stare at each other. How drained we all look!

The rain has stopped, but now and then new clouds float into view. We are all too weary and nervous to talk. Will we have to go through this again tonight?

APRIL 20

We're in luck. The stars are back in the sky. We can doze off leaning against a tree.

Morning. Our faces have cleared up too. We unpack our things and set them out to dry in the sun, which almost overpowers us with its warmth, and we fall asleep again against a tree trunk.

This dreamy restfulness, which lasts half a day, is suddenly shattered by a startling sound: human footsteps on dry twigs. Like poisoned mice, we run back into our hole and stretch out on the ground. Through openings in our shelter we can see a man walking in a semicircle. He pauses at a tree. He coughs. He seems to be telling us: "You might as well come out. I know where you are!"

Our faces grow pale as death. A minute passes. Five. An hour.

How can we possibly know how long we have been lying there without moving, like corpses?

We must do something. We go over all his movements. It seems he has not noticed our presence. But can we gamble on that? The wisest course would be to get away from here. But where would we go? Again, we place ourselves in the hands of fate. We wait. Every passing hour gives us new hope. It was nothing, we console ourselves, but we can't fool our hearts.

Again we divide into optimists and pessimists. The latter can torture you to death. "He must have seen us. The cough was a joke. Why was he examining the area so closely? Why did he stop at that tree?" The optimists naturally find answers to all these questions to produce a favorable result.

People condemned to death. Who has the right to deprive them of the only thing that sustains them—hope? If not for that hope, how could people have survived in the ghetto and the forest? Can we appreciate how great a part Jewish faith has played in Jews' survival? In the Kovno Ghetto there was only one suicide in three years! Compare that to the mass suicides of Jews in Germany, whose experiences up until the deportations were child's play compared to ours. Why? Because in this group of Lithuanian Jews, Jewish faith—the traditional Jewish hopefulness was more animated, more comforting, more supportive. This hope, on the eve of the years of death, took many forms—a revolution in Berlin, German defeats on the war fronts, a Jewish state, and so forth. Its deeper meaning was: "Jews! Do not despair!" So who would dare laugh at the optimists? Often, in the ghetto, one could hear the most foolish words from optimists about politics, war, etc. Who has the right to steal the delusion from a terminally ill patient that he will recover and live a long life? Are consoling hopes for such patients a lesser remedy than a remedy for those who have a curable sickness? Therefore, I simply could not tolerate the pessimists with their clever talk, with their account books in their hands, unfeeling merchants who have no idea of their people's psychology.

So here too I look with revulsion at the pessimists, the defeatists, and let myself be carried away on the wings of hope—hope that today's events will also end well. With silent prayers in our hearts and with awe in our souls we go to bed.

APRIL 21

A restless night. Every so often we poke each other: "Well? Anyone out there?" Finally, when the sun greets the morning and all is quiet, we reassure ourselves that last night's incident is behind us.

It is now six months since we left the ghetto. Sad thoughts about ourselves, about acquaintances, about close friends. A couple of months ago we hoped that at this anniversary we would be closer to liberation. Well, what's done is done. The months that are already behind us are found months. Tomorrow? "About tomorrow let God worry," says the Yiddish adage. There's no other course for us now.

Even at its darkest, life demands its due. For three weeks now we haven't changed our underwear. Pharaoh's third plague is in full force. We are practically skinning ourselves alive. Shamelessly we rub our backs against the tree trunks, like pigs without a fence. We search for the little creatures several times a day. But it doesn't help much. When shall we have the privilege of a bath?

Today the old man pays us a visit, and we forget all our other worries. Obviously drunk, he tells us that he has just come from Antanas's house. Antanas is still locked up for sheltering Jews. His wife is complaining bitterly that despite the generous ransom she has paid, they are still holding him. Who knows whether they will ever release him? "Maybe I should turn them in, the few Jews that I'm hiding, and save my husband's life?" she said to Tadeusz.

The old man tells us that her words upset him so much that he practically yelled at her: "If you do that, I personally will stick a knife into you and your parents! How can you even think of killing so many poor souls?"

Hearing these words, we feel as if paralysis has set in. We have heard the same kind of talk before from the old man, but his tone had not been as serious, and the form was different too. It had sounded more like a passing thought than a well-thought-out plan.

The "righteous among the nations"? Those words should not be used lightly. Only in moments of severe trial do we see people as they really are. Times when everything comes easy, when one is not in any danger, when one is earning money and can even enjoy life—well, all is right. But when the hour of danger is near, that's when a person's courage is really tested.

Philosophy aside, his words about "turning us in" hang over our heads like a sword. We ask him to go back and explain to Antanas's wife that what she has in mind would only make matters worse for her husband—that it would mean certain death.

Again we consider whether we should run away from there, far away, so that neither the old man nor Antanas's wife would know where we were. But after many "on the one hands" and "on the other hands," we decide to wait until we hear what the second round of talks between them will bring. Our lives are in their hands.

APRIL 22

Yesterday's news has left us feeling hopeless. We talk very little. To spite us, the sun has hidden itself behind large dark clouds. Even worse, today for the first time we hear an ominous sound—the thud of an axe against a tree trunk. Somewhere they are chopping down trees. How far away? In the forest, an echo is always loud and can deceive the ear. It does seem, however, that it is not far away because now and then we seem to hear human voices. The continuous chopping sound unnerves us even further. When the old man returns, however, we relax a bit. This time he has brought with him a pot of soup. For over a week now we have not tasted hot soup, so it is a bit of a celebration. We turn all our attention to the meal. The soup sends a warm feeling through our limbs and puts a more relaxed look over everyone's face. We cannot thank the old man enough for his good deeds.

We are so relaxed that we lie down and tell each other stories. Out of our treasure of memories we fish out simple, innocent tales or even light criminal stories. They soothe the nerves. We listen with the rapt attention of naive young children not at the brink of death but safe in their own beds in a Lithuanian shtetl long ago.

The human soul is apparently capable of the strangest transitions.

The only unmarried woman among us, Nechama, has lately begun studying herself in her mirror. This was brought on by a compliment from the old man, who told her that she is looking prettier now that she has been out in the open air. Come to think of it, she was not so sparing of her mirror even before this. After each moment of crisis, out comes her mirror. A woman remains a woman, always and everywhere. I recall a story about a woman whose last request, before they put her on the scaffold, was for a mirror. A man cannot understand this; he will never fathom it.

It seems that our present circumstances provide fertile soil for superstitions. It is amazing how people who in normal times were far removed from such things will let themselves be taken in by all sorts of irrational notions. It doesn't matter that with your common sense and your conscious mind you dismiss them here too. Beneath the threshold of perceptions you long to hear all the magic formulas, and you believe in them. Expressions like "*k'n'ayn'ahoreh*" ("no evil eye"), "*kholile*" ("God forbid"), or "*al tiftakh peh l'sotn*" ("don't give Satan an opening")—expressions like these accompany every word in the mouths of people who would normally have avoided them.

To the list of these superstitions one must add the magical séances that the women keep holding one after another. All the painful problems we are faced with are solved by drawing lots with pine needles—yes-no-yes-no. But even he who does not believe in such nonsense, who mocks it, cannot resist asking: "Well, how did it come out? Yes or no?"

Just dreams, of course. That goes without saying. Our Barbora is a certified interpreter of dreams. She knows "for sure" that dreams about a naked person signify misfortune. Dirty water means sorrow. A dog that bites means an enemy, and so forth. If you dream about clean water, that's a good sign. Fire is good luck. White underwear is also a good sign.

Not a morning goes by that the women do not tell each other their dreams. They remember every little detail. Do not dare question their interpretations or they will present you with a long list of dreams that have proved their assertions.

Doesn't this testify to the inclination of ordinary people toward the transcendental not by way of intellect but rather through the emotions? A tendency toward piety is now also noticeable among people who have lived all their lives without religion.

Our former Jewish plutocrat, a professed atheist if ever there was one, took me aside today and said, "Listen. I've been thinking that a religious person is happier than a nonbeliever. Even his family life is much cleaner. Take me, for instance. I've enjoyed every beautiful woman I've ever wanted. And what remains of that a minute later? Pfui!" And he spat. Then he asked me, "What do you think?"

What should I have told him? Not only moral and spiritual vulgarians like him but also more culturally and morally chaste people are served by religion as a place of refuge in the most difficult moments of their lives. In our circumstances here in the forest, one begins to understand the reason for the stories about atheists who summon a rabbi or priest to their deathbeds. In our present condition of proximate death there is a tremendous craving for spirituality, for a higher, supernatural force, so one raises one's eyes heavenward. In such a situation the most convinced Marxist will never find comfort in a verse from Marx, but the exalted word of a prophet has more than once appeared on the lips of a nonbeliever and, at least for the moment, soothed his burdened spirit. It is astounding how often enlightened, free-thinking people will use the word "God" in hours of mortal danger—and "God" is a word that was once unfit and forbidden to them in normal times.

This is reflected in miniature in our little forest community. In hours of danger, when despair begins to take over, one does not seek comfort in economic principles, nor even in the words of the great poets, but in the Bible. Is man still so small that he must have a God up on high? Or is God so big that man wants to be close to Him?

One can indeed stammer a few words about God and remain the same repulsive character when a moment later the subject changes to earthly matters. A few weeks ago our plutocrat received a few bags of flour from Antanas's wife. In the very difficult days of our wandering around the woods, Tadeusz baked some bread for us. Today the plutocrat asked me, "When will we settle our accounts for the bread?"

The old Lithuanian, who has been sharing with us the meager quota of bread he receives from the Vilkija city administration, has never asked us for a bread accounting. But a Jew, who was still rich even now, demands that a Jewish family living on miracles should "settle accounts for the bread"!

APRIL 28

Another week of forest life has gone by without any worrisome surprises. The weather is not perfect. Sun and clouds, sun and clouds, like a horse race. At night, pack up and run for the tall trees. But it could be worse. Much worse.

Recently, along with the warm weather, some new tenants have moved in with us: birds. Birds of all descriptions. With each morning, even before the sun rises, comes a chirping and a whistling and a warbling, as if the heavens had opened. There are birds of the most varied species here. In the city we never saw them. And when they all start speaking at once, you might as well stuff your ears with cotton. Raja would stone me if she heard me say that. She says that what we are hearing are glorious symphonic arrangements of all these bird tunes. But each tune separately is pretty, and at least it's new to city ears.

Here a bird is singing some kind of prayer. To whom? Another birdsong that sounds just like a whistle has frightened us on more than one occasion. Here is one that sounds like tinkling bells. This bird is a real composer. He not only whistles; he also sounds like a drum. Now you can hear a real goat bleat coming from the throat of one bird. Now a dove is *tra-la-la-ing*, and near him another dove is cooing a mournful tune. All around us there is a chirping and a whistling and a drumming and a ringing—a whole orchestra of musical instruments! Not everyone understands this music, but you can't help listening to it.

So it is no wonder that today Raja reveals to us the secret that she has been listening closely to the conversations of the birds and she now understands their language. She knows that a certain chirp repeated three times is an invitation. Six times from another bird means the invitation has been accepted. And so on. Apparently, the story about King Solomon understanding the language of the birds and animals is not a legend. If he ever had to deal with as many birds as we do here in the forest, he would have displayed the same mastery in this field as the woman here with us.

So far this place is all right, provided we are not given the opportunity to learn the language of the wild beasts. First, that would be a lot more dangerous. And second, we hope we won't be here that long.

MAY 1

Precisely on the first day of this spring month, nature brings us a surprising gift: snow! Winter snow. The look of the forest changes in the blink of an eye. All the trees suddenly start to bloom in white and green. Delightful! Winter and summer meet unexpectedly and kiss, a feat of magic by the most skillful practitioner in the universe. We all stand and gawk at this extraordinary, blinding painting done by nature.

The spectacular show doesn't last long, however. On one side of the sky, blue is breaking through. The snowflakes start to melt. But then, incredibly, the trees seem to be on fire! Yes, electric lights hang from the trees and shower us with sparks. Some of the lights are crystalline white, others blue, others green. Still others are bright red and all the colors of the rainbow. But all together the effect is one of fire. A fascinating picture created by the sun's rays in the drops of water hanging on the branches. The color depends on the direction of the rays and from what angle you are viewing the display. A marvelous picture; you cannot take your eyes off of it. After a while, the fires burn out, like meteors.

MAY 3

The sky is clouding up. The sun is playing hide and seek. But now we have a new worry. The first illness since we came into the forest. The patient, a woman of about fifty-five, is burning up with over 104 degrees of fever. What are we to do? To add to the problem, there is a sudden downpour. Even the tall trees cannot protect us from a rain like this. The woman is curled up under blankets, covered with grass and surrounded by shrubs. Her face is covered with a raincoat. She doesn't move a muscle. A corpse. All that's missing is the black cloth. We have no medicine. No food. What to do?

"How goodly are thy tents, O Jacob!" In my mind's eye I can see the large letters of this blessing in my childhood prayer book. How ironic these words sound here under the open sky, with the rain pouring down on this sick woman and on us. "*Ashreynu*—how goodly is our portion!"

Whenever we were driven out or persecuted, we beat our breasts and said "*Oshomnu*"—we have sinned. When our enemies enjoyed a sunny life as we languished in the ghetto, we sang "*Ashreynu!*"—an extraordinary nation! Faith is the answer to all questions. When will our "avenging God" come and give his lost, sinful children a roof over their heads?

MAY 4

The woman's temperature is still over 104 degrees. There is nothing left for us to do but take her back to the cottage without asking permission from the old couple. Since we have no other choice, we do it.

Lately the old man has been telling us stories in which Jews are turned in. Today he informs us that several months ago a peasant agreed to take in two young Jewish children. He even favored them with a new religion. But then he lost his nerve and left them at the door of a church. The children were taken to a Lithuanian children's home, where their identity was discovered. When the Lithuanian partisans got wind of this they went to the home, took the two children into the forest, and shot them.

Another of the old man's stories is about a Jewish girl who had been hidden for three years by a young Lithuanian. The girl paid for this privilege with her body. Whether this was payment to him for risking his life or whether he was in love with her I do not know. But there was another young Lithuanian man there, a brother. He too wanted to enjoy this young woman. He reasoned that he too was risking his life so he too had a right to his share. His threats about turning her in were not taken seriously by his brother until one day two Lithuanian policemen came, shot the girl, and hanged her lover.

People betrayed, people turned in—is our turn coming?

MAY 10

For ten days in a row we have not had a day without some rain. It pours; sometimes it merely drizzles. Regardless, it does not let up. For four days the sky has been a mass of black clouds. For nine nights we have not slept lying down. Our bones feel as if they are about to break. Everybody has a headache. No one has any dry clothes left to change into.

All bent over, we lean against the tree trunks. What can we do during such hours? One of us fantasizes out loud: "If a British plane landed here now to pick us up, would you risk it?" We see no tragedy in such a question. We discuss the problem as if we really had to make a decision about getting on that British plane.

It helps us when we do this sort of thing.

When you fly up to heaven you forget about the earth. Fantasy swallows up reality for a while, leaving less room for horror and pain.

"Let's say I'm building castles in the air. Let's say the world doesn't even exist. In my dreams I feel better and brighter. In my dreams the skies are much bluer." Once upon a time this was for us only a sentimental song. Now it is the deeper melody of our soul.

Strange. That same question—"What would we do if a friendly plane suddenly appeared here?"—was once raised in all seriousness at a meeting of the Central Committee of the Socialist Zionists in the ghetto. Around the table sat people who, before the catastrophe, were leading personalities in the communal-political life of Jewish Lithuania. But no one cast any suspicious glances at the questioner, as if he had suddenly lost his mind. No. We interrupted the previous debate and began discussing the new question.

One wants to flee from horrible surroundings. If we can't do it through the barbed wire, we do it through the imagination. Imagination was a great treasure in the ghetto. It's the same in the forest.

Whoever has not been blessed with the ability to lift himself up on the wings of fantasy has nothing left but the curse of literally eating himself up alive. How long can a person live with only constant thoughts of death?

I knew a man in the ghetto who saw the situation very clearly and sharply. Whenever anyone interpreted an event in a way that did not coincide with his utterly logical conception about the ultimate destruction of the ghetto, he would call that person a "foolish fantasizer." He was much too learned and much too clever to occupy himself with such foolish dreams. He saw the situation so clearly that he went out of his mind. His endless thoughts of gloom engulfed him until he was consumed by his own inner fire.

The wings of fantasy in the ghetto and the forest were wings of life.

MAY 11

This morning brings us the best news possible: white and blue streaks appear in the sky. In the east the horizon reddens, and the sun comes promenading out. We run out from beneath the trees whose trunks we have been hugging for ten days and ten nights and go forth to welcome the shining princess. At first she receives us coolly, but with each passing hour her rays grow warmer and warmer. Our mood changes. We bring out our old clothing and bedclothes and hang them out, as we used to do in the small towns before Passover. Now when the rain comes at least there will be a dry shirt to put on.

MAY 13

A few days of sunshine and warmth. Like a lover who has been separated from his beloved, we cannot contain our joy on seeing the sun again.

But then the mood is changed again by the arrival of a very frightened Barbora. "No one has been here looking for you?" she demands.

A little bit later Tadeusz comes and asks the same question: "Are you sure no strangers have been here?"

What sort of question is that? No one is even supposed to know where we are. Have they made some kind of deal with Antanas's wife to carry out her plans for us? Meanwhile the old woman has been taking things from us left and right. Lately she has taken a fancy to everything she sees: the colored kerchief, the silk dress, the embroidered towel. Not at all like the old "Mamita," as we used to call her.

How difficult it is to live at someone's mercy. "Do not leave us to depend on the largesse of flesh and blood." How much more so when it's a matter not of bread but of life and death.

MAY 14

The question of bread is still the most pressing. Three days a week we can't have any at all. And the rest of the time it is doled out piecemeal. So again we must take the big risk: Nechama and Mr. F will go into the neighborhood and trade our personal belongings for food.

Soon after they leave we hear footsteps. Animals? Humans? A loud sneeze and a snort answer our question. A horse has come to pay us a social call. There is grass in the forest, so the peasants send their animals out to graze. Is the horse alone or is someone with him? We look through the cracks. Nothing is visible. We stretch out on the ground, our only means of protection, and we wait, our hearts beating like trip-hammers. The horse continues to announce his presence, but there is still no sign of a human being. What to do? Drive the animal away? Suppose we send it in the wrong direction? We come to a decision: we put fresh leaves on all the paths that we have made with our own feet.

With heavy hearts we go to sleep and wish to each other that when we wake up in the morning we will no longer have a horse as a neighbor. The horse is okay, but what about his owner?

MAY 15

The sun is warmer every day. The weather is turning hot. By afternoon it's steaming. We throw off some of our rags—the double coat, the double pants, the double underwear, and the double socks. In the last couple of days the forest has burgeoned and become one big blossom. Buds and leaves and flowers of all sorts. Blinding colors. The scent is tangy, overpowering. Orphaned trees show off their new bird's nests. Their green limbs now sway with springtime festivity. For us the foliage has another special virtue: it makes the forest denser and provides better cover for our place of refuge.

The warm weather has solved some of our problems, but they are immediately replaced by new ones. First, a plague of gnats. They are such tiny creatures with shriveled legs, but still they attack with a ferocity that is unbearable. All of us are covered with their bites. They plunge their needles right through our socks. The white dots with the red circles that appear on the skin after one of their bites are terribly itchy. What's more, they attack with a loud buzz that is unnerving. Apparently this is a means of frightening and confusing their victims. Also, they don't seem to need much sleep, because even at night we have no relief from their activity. The only relief comes during the few cool hours in the early morning.

This is only the beginning, Tadeusz and Barbora tell us. Later they will attack in droves. Armies of them. But you have to take the optimistic view: no matter how hard they bite, they can't kill you!

The early hot spell brings us another concern: our little stream has practically dried up. The bit of water that's left cannot be used for drinking; it is yellow, dirty, and full of worms. Nor will any amount of sifting help. So now we are dependent on the old man for water too and must use it very sparingly, the same as we do with the bread.

For three days Tadeusz has not been here. Fear, doubts, worry. We comfort ourselves with the hope that soon our two emissaries will be returning from their "business trip" to the surrounding villages. But this is already the third day, and there's no sign of them. With every passing hour our uneasiness mounts.

At such agonizing moments one seeks a little solace in the Book of Books. What other book is so suited for this, especially for one who, in his childhood, absorbed into his soul not only the words and ideas but also its sounds and its rhythms? But where is one to find this book? One recalls only disconnected verses. I can't forgive myself for forgetting to take along a Bible. I must be satisfied now with the only Jewish book here—a small Rosh Hashanah prayer book.

How many years is it since I last looked into it? How long is it since I last set foot in a synagogue? Yet how familiar it still is, how touching, how comforting every word sounds. And after all, what is more suited to us now than a "*zokhreynu l'khayim*" ("remember us for life") or a "*z'khor rakhmekho*" ("remember thy mercy") or an "*ovinu malkeynu*" ("Our Father Our King") and similar prayers? As if they had been written in our own cruel time and especially for us.

How many memories of childhood are awakened by every word and every melody that you cannot forget, that you take with you into the grave? Comrades, friends, parents, the old shtetl with all its characters and customs—rabbis, cantors, ritual animal slaughterers, Hebrew teachers, gabbais, your first teachers, wagon drivers, butchers; Friday nights, Sabbath eves, holidays, weekdays, music-filled weddings, and mournful funerals.

The instinct for life, on its untrodden, overgrown paths, is driving us to the sea of old memories, and again and again we ask ourselves, in anger and misery: "*Ad mosay*"—"How much longer, O Lord, how much longer?"

MAY 16

With the morning came our two emissaries. Bone-weary, muddy, bedraggled, the Eternal Wanderers in the flesh. More than once they had lost their way in the forest jungle. With their arrival, however, our mood changes too. Two loaves of bread, some butter, a hunk of meat, and in addition a whole pack of old newspapers—what more could we have hoped for? The old man visits us today too. We present him with some food and he too becomes a new man. For some reason he doesn't say anything at all about spies today, or about captured Jews. "Tis better to give than to receive . . ."

MAY 24

Eight days later we must again lift the bundles onto our shoulders and go forth upon our perilous journey.

We are no longer five but three, which has deepened our gloom. Under such circumstances you look for ways to forget your troubles, and if you look for something you usually find it. On the branches of our "bunker" we set out a few crumbs for the birds. The cowardly ones are fools, but the bolder ones move quickly, orient themselves, and get what they want. Soon they even begin eating out of our hands. What pretty little creatures! Tiny, with dark heads and white neck bands, with blue wings and red dots. Aside from the crumbs they also take a fancy to the fur that we cover ourselves with at night. They swoop down, land with both feet, and peck at it with a considerable persistence. A soft bed for the little birds! But for us? The skies grow angry with us and punish us with a downpour. A real storm. The tall, slender trees bend almost to the ground. Any minute they will snap in two. Fortunately, they have grown so close together that they can lean on each other in their hour of need. The more violent the storm the smaller and more helpless you feel. The whistling of the wind through the trees is like a thousand wheels rolling over a cobblestone pavement. And all you can do is lean against a tree and tremble.

"Dust you are, and unto dust shall you return." At such moments you feel that truth most sharply and painfully. Is it any wonder that not only idolatrous peoples have deified storms? Highly developed, monotheistic peoples have done the same. With the Jewish people the revelation of God is often associated with thunder and lightning and storms. Even where the highest stage of being is "the still, soft voice of peace," a storm precedes it. At times of frightening natural events, there is still cause for spiritualization. Parallel to deep self-understanding is humble self-deprecation for the simple human being, as well as for the prophet.

So the trees shake and we shake with them. The trees bow and we bow with them, before the earthly forces that create and destroy, build and demolish, give birth and kill, and yet every day renew creation. Forces beyond our knowledge and control remain a mysterious part of struggling mankind.

JUNE 1

The brighter the weather grows and the clearer the skies, the darker grows our situation down below. The fast-growing grasses attract cows. Whole herds of them now venture into the forest. In addition, the farmers often lead them out to the stream not far from us. Each day the situation grows worse, more terrifying.

Today we were on the verge of catastrophe. One herd of cows was heading straight for our refuge. We held our breath and threw ourselves to the ground, like children playing "If I can't see you, you can't see me." Some of us covered our faces with our coats, exactly like my teacher, who used to cover himself with a featherbed during a storm.

As we freeze in that way we suddenly hear a loud breathing close by: a black cow is introducing herself to us in all her glory! Since we hear no humans in the vicinity, we take a chance and shoo the cow away. In the evening, the whole herd comes to visit, but this time we cannot take the risk of leaving our bunker. We try to drive them away with a pole that we have prepared, swinging it around wildly. Like scared mice we scurry around inside our "hut" and keep chasing them—these poor, dumb creatures of whom we are not afraid. What we do fear are the loose tongues of their shepherds and owners.

New guests: dogs. They must belong to the shepherds. Three dogs in a row. Is anyone with them? What shall we do if the dogs start barking and the shepherds follow them right to our spot? Miraculously, the dogs do not bark. But miracles do not happen every day. And to add to the problem, there is a flower growing here that, Barbora told us, is used by the peasants for making medicines, and their season will begin any day now. So again, get up and go. From the forest back to the bushes. Slogging for hours along muddy paths in the dark of night.

JUNE 2

The new place seems to be more isolated than the old one, but it has one serious shortcoming: it is situated about three hundred yards from a house. But what choice do we have? We are not the masters of our fate. We go wherever Tadeusz takes us.

And of course we are welcomed by a downpour. Our protection is a very wide pine tree that turns out to be a veritable umbrella. It is one of a kind among all sorts of very short trees that are more like bushes. One gets the feeling that this big tree was awaiting our arrival, exactly like the ram of Father Abraham at the altar for Isaac.

We lie down to sleep. First night, first alarm. A loud rustle among the trees. As we watch, a large gray-white animal appears. In the half-light we can distinguish a pair of fierce, gleaming eyes. A dog? A wolf? I stand up. The animal does not budge. Nor does it bark. It does not retreat. Can it be one of the two large dogs that belong to the owner of these bushes? They have a reputation in the neighborhood. While we were still living in the stable, Tadeusz had told us many horror stories about them. This time we try a new method—chunks of buttered bread. First he hesitates. Then he succumbs to temptation. A few pieces of bread will keep him quiet. But no sooner does he turn away than a bigger dog takes his place. We try the same method, and it works. The bread is part of our rations, but there is no other way. In an age when Hitler reigns, dogs must have their appetites sated.

JUNE 9

Ants are especially interesting creatures, and the author of the Book of Proverbs knew what he was doing when he sent the lazy boy to watch them and learn their ways. So interesting how they run back and forth, toiling from sunrise to sunset. Not one of them stands idle for a moment. They drag loads much heavier than themselves. They help one another. They carry away their sick and their dead. They do many, many other wondrous things.

But that's only when you pay them a short visit during the day and at night go to sleep in your own bed. When these same ants are under your head, when they crawl ceaselessly over your body, when your food is full of them—then you have very little inclination to study these charming creatures. You want to get as far away from them as possible. Our old friends the gnats do not desert us either, and they are worse than the ants.

Here at our new place there is a more treacherous species than those in the forest, with silver spots on their crooked legs. All day long we keep after them with our fans—twigs with the leaves still attached. This is our only defense against the gnats. Now I understand very clearly why the Creator of the Universe selected the gnat, out of all the other insects, to punish the wicked Titus. We realize that these creatures can actually kill you; they are such persistent nuisances that they can torture a person to death, and even without a special mission from the Heavenly Court!

For that reason, I cannot understand the folk saying "quiet as a gnat" or "it's so quiet you can't even hear a gnat." Apparently, the anonymous authors of the sayings spent all their lives in the city. They never had to wander around lost in the fields and woods. Because it is precisely these tiny creatures that create so much noise around themselves that it is simply astonishing. Where do they get the strength?

Another unwelcome guest is the tick, who burrows under your skin with its head, leaving its rear end on the outside. The bite is painful, and it takes strength and skill to pull the creature out. When you add this fine fellow to the various flies, bees, worms, snakes, and so on that live here in great profusion, you get a picture of the company we keep day and night.

JULY 11

Today, after a few "peaceful" weeks, we are again almost frightened to death. In the evening, as we sit and talk, we hear a rustling in the bushes and assume it is Tadeusz. I go out to meet him on the path—and find a stranger there with a rifle! Even with his nondescript jacket and his torn shirt he looks dangerous. We study each other silently like two wild beasts. I hear Raja and Nechama behind me running and urging me to run too. A minute passes, an eternity, and a thousand thoughts. How can a person have so many thoughts in a single moment? Apparently, before death, the spiritual strength of human beings is magnified. That's why people say that in the final moments before death the events of one's lifetime pass in review. Are these my last moments?

The other man is still standing there motionless. Who is he? What is he likely to do? How can I defend myself? Suddenly he says something—in Russian. "Sit down, sit down, don't be afraid," and he turns and walks away.

Not until that moment do I realize the great danger I have been in. My wife has fainted. Her sister looks pale as a corpse. Do we have to move again now?

Before we can get our bundles together a familiar figure appears. It is Moyshe, one of those eight of us who had started out together. He tells us that the man I met was a guest of the peasant who owns these bushes. He had gone out to hunt rabbits. He feels bad that he alarmed us, and he has sent along a bottle of milk and some fresh turnips.

How many years have these few moments taken off our lives?

When we recover a bit, we ask Moyshe why he left his last hiding place and moved here.

This is his story.

He had been hiding in a specially camouflaged little room in the house. One night he had felt as if he were suffocating in these tight quarters, so he left quietly and went up to the attic in the barn. In the morning he heard the following conversation down below: "I like that watch he's wearing."

"Ask him for it."

"What if he doesn't give it to me?"

"What?"

"You hear what I said."

"How much longer do you think he's going to live? Who knows whether the Russians will ever come here?"

"And suppose he still refuses to give it to me?"

"Don't worry, there's always a way . . ."

Several hours after this dreadful conversation, our friend tells us, the peasant comes in and says: "You know, Mikolas, what happened the other day to one of your people? Someone in a nearby village offered to hide him. The next morning he said to him: 'You never know what can happen to Jews nowadays! You never know. Why don't you write your will so your brother in America will know your wishes. Say that if you don't survive, he should send your money to me.' The Jew made out such a will, and the day after he wrote it he was already six feet under.

"When I heard that story I felt as if my head was coming off. I began to sense the murderous thoughts of my host and I began to understand that a place in the ground was being prepared for me too. That same night I ran away and came here to Maximas, who agreed to take me in."

JULY 19

The last few days we've been hearing the music of liberation, the thunder and lightning of bombs and cannon fire. It's frightening and it's unsettling, yet we wait impatiently for every explosion. When it stops for a moment, our hearts seem to grow heavier.

Three years ago, when the Germans were preparing to march into Kovno, the Lithuanian newspapers wrote similar lines about "the music of liberation"—I am quoting it verbatim from a Lithuanian newspaper that characterized the German bombs in that way. The Lithuanian papers wrote about how the Lithuanians, with tears of joy in their eyes, went out to welcome their German "liberators." And now we are experiencing similar feelings about the Russians. Times do change . . .

We have absolutely no idea what's going on in the world. The only news we get are the dull detonations and explosions. In the evening we can hear machine gun clatter. German or Russian? Is the front truly that close to us? The heart beats faster.

The Lithuanians weep bitter tears. The old man tells us that they are deathly afraid of the approaching Russian army.

"Why are you afraid?" he had asked a neighbor.

"The Russians will slaughter every last one of us."

"Are there any partisans in your family?"

"No."

"Then why are you afraid? The Russians don't harm innocent people."

"Yes, but our partisans didn't differentiate between the guilty and the innocent. Why should the Russian partisans do otherwise?"

Now that the knife is at their own throat, the conscience awakens. Before, they were blind and deaf to the grief and agony of the Jews in their country.

JULY 20

A crackling of twigs once, twice, and before our eyes appears the image of a total stranger: tall, blond, and wearing peasant clothing. Our glances meet for a second, then he turns aside without a word.

Who is he? There is no time to think. We grab our bundles and head for the bushes near the home of the old couple.

Almost immediately there's trouble. We can hear a group of men approaching Tadeusz's house, singing as they go. The dog starts barking his head off. "A heart is like a clock" the saying goes, and our hearts are not announcing any good news. Shall we run away from here again? The problem is that Nechama has just gone into the house, and there hasn't been time enough for her to get out. The singing voices are coming closer. We can already make out a word or two of their conversation with Tadeusz.

Shall we stay? Shall we flee?

In the midst of this indecision, Nechama, who had remained in the house, comes out looking like an apparition. She tells us that the old man has run up to the attic.

"Get out! Run to the forest!" he had hissed.

She is so bewildered that she doesn't know whether the strangers were already inside the house when she ran down from the attic. She doesn't know whether they noticed her or not. But from the expression on the old man's face she thinks they must be from the secret service. Three of them. While she had been up in the attic, she noticed that one of them stood in one spot, examining the place as if he were looking for something or someone.

Shall we run? We are three people. Our flight through the bushes will create a lot of noise. The men in the house will surely hear it. We come to a quick decision: to stay where we are. We move carefully to a more protected position, stretch out on the ground, and wait, holding our breath.

Inside the house all is quiet. No yelling, no screaming. A favorable sign. But listen! Something is slithering through the bushes. The sound is moving in our direction. Our limbs feel paralyzed. Is one of those men coming to search the bushes? It's too late now for us to run. We press our faces to the ground and hover between life and death.

Never before have I felt such a strong desire to have a weapon in my hand. Three people lying there like sheep, afraid to move, and only one person, it seems, is moving boldly toward us. The possession of a weapon, I realize for the first time, adds a feeling of security in moments of danger and buoys up your courage. I've never had the occasion before to think about this. I had no concept of such things. I cannot forgive myself for not learning how to use a weapon before we left the ghetto. The good doctor Elijah Segal, himself a former officer and underground leader in the ghetto, had pleaded with me to give him an hour during which he would teach me how to use a revolver. But of what use are regrets now?

In the meantime we are lying here helplessly, waiting for another miracle.

And the miracle happens. When the human ghost comes close to us, it suddenly turns and moves in another direction. We can hear footsteps receding, receding, until we can no longer hear them at all. But we stay put for a long time. We do not move until we are certain. Then we raise our heads a little and straighten out our limbs.

The momentary danger is over. But who was it? And where are the others? To go into the cottage now would be a great risk. But we must find out. Luckily, night has fallen, and for a few hours at least we'll be safe. In the dark murderers are afraid to slink around in such places. But with all our hearts we wish such happy nights on Hitler and his gang of cutthroats.

CHAPTER 6

A Visitor From The Ghetto

JULY 21

It is now almost a month since the Soviet offensive started on "our" front. Now we are even more isolated from the world than we were before because we haven't seen any kind of newspapers. We get our news from the old man.

Our only source of information: the artillery bombardments. From the first moment they reached our ears we knew for certain that the front is moving closer to us. Every salvo awakens new hope. Our days now are occupied in trying to guess the distance according to the force of the salvos.

Today, however, it has been quiet. This makes us uneasy. Has something happened? Was the Red Army being pushed back? Only recently we learned that Vilna was liberated. What about Kovno? There was news that fighting is going on in the suburbs. If that's true, we should be hearing intensified firing now, but instead things have grown quieter.

Today, in this mood of tense expectation of world-shaking events, we have a visitor—a man who escaped from the Kovno ghetto three weeks ago. He brings us the latest news from the ghetto, but it is all bad. What other kind of news could he have brought us from the Valley of Death?

First he gives us shocking details about the cruelest of all the "actions"—deporting the children from the ghetto. More important than the details, it seems to me, is their psychological background. How fiendishly slick the children's "action" was! Wilhelm Göcke, the hangman of many Jewish ghettos, is very cunning, an expert in psychology. Craftily he carried out his murderous plan in a "peaceful" manner, lulling the attention of the Jewish leaders. He did this in such a sadistically clever way that even now there are Jews who regard him as a "good German" and even a friend of the Jews! A legend is already circulating that he actually postponed the children's "action" for four or five months . . .

But only naive and gullible people can think like that about this ultra-clever German sadist. Göcke is one of those sophisticated murderers who is always much more dangerous than the simple ones. He lived on blood and for blood—and gave the impression of being sympathetic and merciful. He murdered Jews—and wanted to be remembered by their survivors as a friend of the Jews. Even with the precious Jewish children, up to the very last moment of killing them, he still played the role of the good uncle, handing out chocolates and other goodies while he turned up the radios in the trucks to drown out their weeping and screaming.

What an art the Germans have made from murdering innocent people!

There were some Jewish mothers for whom it was such a trauma to be separated from their children that they themselves led the children to the trucks. The Germans then sent specially trained dogs at them to bite their hands. There were also good Germans there who found it so trying to witness this grief that they permitted the mothers to ride with their children to a shared death.

How fiendishly evil people have become when its sons are characterized as "good" because they "permitted" mothers to go to the slaughter with their children!

The children's "action" is probably the worst of all the calamities the ghetto was forced to endure. In previous "actions" (such as deporting ten thousand people at a time) there was still room for hope and self-deception, even though people did not want to believe and didn't know for certain that what was happening was literally mass genocide. The children's "action," however, was clearly 100 percent slaughter. There was no place for the slightest belief of the craziest optimists—of whom there were more than a few in the ghetto and who even played a positive role at times during those awful ghetto years.

In this kind of obvious mass extermination, Jewish mothers

carried their children to the slaughterer, and not even one of them tried to throw a stone. This is a terrible thing to say, and it is absolutely incomprehensible. A hen, when a bird of prey approaches to steal her chicks, tries to peck with her beak; a cat tries to scratch the abductor of her kittens; but Jewish mothers, among the finest mothers in the world, led their dearest ones to the slaughter without any resistance whatsoever. A very small number tried to go with their children and die with them, but almost no one offered even as much resistance as a mother cat would have!

The Jews in the ghetto were one large hypnotized mass. How many times did every one of us in the ghetto feel that we did not even have the strength to move a finger? Imagine a situation where you must run if you want to escape from the Angel of Death—but your feet refuse to move. They are paralyzed by fear. Can you condemn a man who does not flee from death because his legs were taken from him? How could the paralyzed hands of a mother pull her child out of the grasp of the slaughterer?

To this purely psychological condition one must add the crafty, sadistic system of the Germans, which pulverized the ghetto Jews morally and spiritually. This system worked. It did what it was supposed to do. And even the Jewish mother—the most beautiful jewel in the crown of the Jewish family—became its victim. All her emotions were atrophied. The effect of the invisible but ever-flowing Hitler poison in the hearts and minds of the ghetto Jews revealed itself also in the acts of the dear mothers. In a perpetual daze, they put their most precious possessions directly into the hands of the murderers.

Were Jewish mothers in the ghetto not poisoned and paralyzed when, in the beginning, they carried their dead children to the cemetery? I myself heard mothers say—as they were returning from the funerals of their babies—"maybe it's better this way." Is there a deeper, more monstrous, more ghastly tragedy than the tragedy of the Jewish mother in the ghetto?

Even Dr. Elkes, the head of the Judenrat, placed a little too much trust in this Göcke. The crafty German hangman understood exactly how to handle that honest but politically naive doctor. He would even visit Elkes at his home. A high officer of the Master Race in the home of a Jew! This was a tremendous surprise to everyone and had a powerful effect on the Jewish leader. After one of those private visits, Dr. Elkes shared his impressions with a circle of close friends. A man like Göcke, he said, would not harm the ghetto on his own initiative. When Elkes's cousin asked him what he should do about his child, for whom he had a hiding place prepared in a village, the Judenrat leader replied that if he had a completely trustworthy peasant he should entrust the child to him, but if not he should keep the child at home because the Jewish children were in no danger.

This was only a short time before the children were deported.

The climax of Göcke's sadism came when the Russians were approaching Lithuanian territory. The only hope for the ghetto was a Russian breakthrough at the front or a revolution in Germany. When neither of those things happened, it became clear that the end of the ghetto was near. The ghetto became a real cemetery. People looked like shadows. They ran around like rats in a trap with only one prospect: death.

Göcke told Dr. Elkes: "Inform your Jews that they have nothing to fear. If the front lines come too close to Lithuanian territory, the ghetto will be evacuated. Transport vehicles will be used for the weaker people, and I myself will lead the others out of the ghetto like Moses did with the Jews of Egypt. Inside Germany we will set up a new labor camp where I shall be with you again."

Göcke was a master at confusing people's minds. In the last months of the ghetto's existence he often interceded for Jews who were caught committing various "crimes" and put in jail. His intercession, of course, meant that the transgressors were released. Clearly this was a well-thought-out plan—either by him or by the Gestapo itself. The relief of the Jews and their families who were temporarily spared this way beclouded people's minds and prevented them from understanding in time the true purpose of this fiendish trick. Confidence in this clever murderer continued to grow.

Calculating, with diabolical intent, was also the "order" he established in the economic life of the ghetto when he arrived there. He paid no attention to a previous ruling that Jews were not permitted to use money. He also closed his eyes to the packages that Jews brought back with them from the city. He must have thought that if they had enough to eat, the Jews in the ghetto would not notice other things that he was doing. He increased the rations. During his term potatoes were so plentiful that people could not use them all. Moldy bread lay in the breadboxes.

Marmalade, butter, even sugar were provided with a generous hand. Equally treacherous were his tactics in the large workshops where some 2,500 Jews were laboring. He gave them orders that were unusually large even for normal times and could have supplied work for many months after the war. From his viewpoint this approach was correct, psychologically well founded. Many Jews let themselves be misled by these tricks and did not try to save themselves by escaping from the ghetto in time.

JULY 22

The man from the Slabodka Ghetto who had accidentally stumbled upon us told us again today about the arrest of the Judenrat members and also of the social authority and the housing department. They had been taken to the Ninth Fort on April 4, 1944, and they all came out of the experience alive, but his description of the behavior of Dr. Elkes is worth recording. In the car going to the fort, from which no one had the slightest hope of returning, Dr. Elkes cited several occasions in Jewish history when leaders died bravely for their people. He placed special emphasis on the Ten Martyrs in Roman times who had been executed by the government. He encouraged and strengthened his associates as they stared into the face of death.

But not only toward the Jews did Dr. Elkes exhibit so strong a stance and attitude. The German executioners too admired his Maccabean spirit and had a good time laughing at it. Our informant is not acquainted with the entire conversation between Dr. Elkes and his Gestapo inquisitors in the Ninth Fort, but the two questions and answers which he did report to us give the reader a good idea of its nature:

Gestapo: What is your worldview?

National Jew.

Gestapo: What do you mean by that?

A Jew with a past and a future.

Gestapo: And what do those words signify?

The Land of Israel!

Our informant also tells us that a week earlier, at the Ninth Fort, most of the Jewish ghetto police, in the face of death and under the most excruciating Gestapo torture, had not betrayed their brothers. The strongest was Moyshe Levin, the last chief of the ghetto police in Slabodka, who defied his tormentors up until the last moment, when a bullet put an end to his life.

Concerning Moyshe Levin, there is more to tell. He had many critics in the ghetto, even in the leading circles of the Zionist underground. His actions in the final months of his duties as police chief, especially in his last hours at the Ninth Fort, are a warning as to how careful one must be when judging people who were in leading positions in the ghettos.

For many Jews in the ghetto, the name "Moyshe Levin" was unfamiliar, even after he became chief of police. He was known to everyone as "de Gaulle" because of his firm, strong hand. During his first two years in the ghetto the responsible circles in and around the Judenrat did not think very highly of him. For that reason, they moved him from post to post. For a time, he was chief of the criminal police in the ghetto—a fifth rank organization—with the clear intention that he would not be able to interfere in anything and would know nothing about the important and often secret tasks the general Jewish police had to carry out. Then he was taken back into the regular ghetto police. At that time, if the Jews had been more decisive and courageous, they would not have allowed him to hold any position in the police or in any other ghetto institution. It was his brother-in-law, the attorney Goldberg, a leading member of the Judenrat, who came to his aid.

Perhaps there was an even stronger force at work. I remember very well that in the Central Committee of the Socialist Zionists they often talked about possible connections between Moyshe Levin and the Gestapo—the go-between being Kaspi Serebrowicz, the Jewish Gestapo agent in Kovno. (For the sake of speaking carefully, one should find another way to characterize this former director of the Hebrew Tarbut school in Telšiai, a leading member of the Lithuanian Revisionists, and a Kovno Yiddish journalist who lived outside the ghetto with his wife and children. But judgment about his personality and actions—that should be left to those who were often forced to meet with this representative of the Gestapo, who was later shot by the Gestapo along with the rest of his family.)

Not until Moyshe Levin became chief of the Jewish ghetto police did leading circles of the ghetto begin to change their opinion about him. (And there can be no doubt that the Judenrat had nothing to do with his appointment.) One can only imagine how tough it was to be the chief of the Jewish police if one did not wish to be merely an agent of the Gestapo. This was especially difficult in the final year. On the one hand he had to carry out the orders of the Nazi authorities; on the other hand, he had to protect the Jews however possible. In this difficult period, there were those came to reflect positively on his character.

When the Gestapo took the few hundred Jewish police officers to the Fort on March 27—after long hours of torture on the square across from Nazi headquarters—Levin told them that he did not expect to come out alive. He told them not to give away any secrets and that, in any case, they must place the blame on him and in that way could perhaps save their own lives.

One of the policemen had proposed that they overpower the guards and escape into the forest with the trucks. That kind of operation had a chance of succeeding, even though they were being followed by a car full of armed Germans. In every truck there were 30 or 40 young, strong Jewish policemen, guarded by only two or three Germans, who were not in a good position to fire their weapons. Some of the policemen would certainly have been able to escape in the ensuing confusion.

Moyshe Levin opposed this plan, however. He argued that such an attack would result in the immediate destruction of the ghetto and that, not being prepared, no one would have the least chance to escape. Thus, the plan was abandoned. The Jewish policemen were incarcerated and except for a few, they did not survive.

After that, there were not many details reported about Moyshe Levin. He was called in first and was brutally tortured for secrets about the ghetto, partisans, hiding places, and so on. According to reports, his only answer was that he knew nothing.

There were cases that were just the opposite of the way Moyshe Levin behaved. Some individuals who had been idealists in the early days of the ghetto fell so low at critical moments that they became spies and informers.

One of them was the ghetto policeman Sergei. Like Levin, he was one of the Revisionist leaders in the ghetto, a member of the Executive Committee of the small Revisionist circle. All its secret tasks were entrusted to him. For a long time there had been a radio in his room; only a select few of the circle knew about it. In all the critical moments of the ghetto you could see Sergei walking through all the narrow streets, patrolling and carrying out various important tasks for the ghetto. He also had a hand in the purchase and hiding of weapons. He was present at all the military resistance exercises of the Jewish underground in the ghetto.

But at the most critical moment he failed the test. Along with other Jewish police who were in his cell in the fort, he began a rebellion against Moyshe Levin, his chief, and against Levin's order not to reveal any secrets. In exchange for a Gestapo promise to spare their lives, Sergei and others betrayed important ghetto information. The Jewish police, especially such trustworthy people as Sergei, knew where the most important hiding places of individuals and organizations were. The "bunkers" were one of the strongest links in the ghetto defense system against the Gestapo. We believed that when the front moved too close, the Germans would destroy the ghetto, and hence hundreds of thousands of marks were spent in building these bunkers. Some were so well constructed that unless their locations were revealed they would never have been discovered by the Gestapo. But a number were disclosed by Sergei and the other police in his cell, thereby sealing the fate of many Jews in the ghetto.

Thus began the deterioration of such a nationally conscious young Jew, until he became an active participant in the official Jewish police informers under the leadership of Arnstein and Grossman. Sergei even made a last-minute attempt to justify his actions: he tried to arrange a conversation with Hirsh Levin, a leader of the Revisionists in the ghetto, but Levin refused to meet with a man who had exposed the ghetto's defenses and thereby the most important interests of his own people.

Our visitor also told us about the end of the concerts in the ghetto.

After the "Great Action" on October 28, 1941, a peaceful period began in the ghetto. Several months passed without any Gestapo raids whatsoever, and in some ways ghetto life returned to normal. Among the normal activities that resumed were the concerts. These were organized with the permission of the Judenrat. The director was the well-known artist Hofmekler, who in former years had conducted the orchestra of the Lithuania State Opera. Playing in the ghetto orchestra were former violinists and conductors like Stupel, Pomerantz, and Vera Schor. The composition of the orchestra guaranteed a high level of performance, but doubts arose as to whether it was even permissible to arrange public concerts in a place from which thousands of Jews had just been led to their death, in a country where 80 percent of the Jewish population had been massacred, at a time when Jewish blood was flowing like water all over Europe.

Since music during a period of mourning had always been banned in Jewish communities, the concerts aroused revulsion in the population. Every man and woman would cover their ears whenever they passed the police building where the concerts were being held, unwilling to listen to any kind of music during the endless shiva days in the ghetto.

The Judenrat and most of the leaders of the ghetto institutions, however, vigorously defended these concerts. They could certainly understand the motives—or more correctly the *feelings*—of those who were opposed to them, but they apparently wished to calm the spirits of the Jews in the ghetto and perhaps turn their interests to higher matters. Since all schools and synagogues and public gatherings were forbidden, they probably believed that in times like these it was permitted to break the strict law of mourning.

Which view was the right one? Did the reasoning of the Judenrat have any merit? The matter of the concerts was part of a more general discussion. It was easier to discuss these views emotionally than rationally!

I can give a personal example of this dilemma. When I had heard the first concert in the ghetto, I was deeply moved. After such personal and national experiences in a Hitlerite Pale of Death, on the fresh graves of family and friends, grimy from laboring on airfields and garbage dumps, insulted and beaten by bullies and two legged beasts—after all this, to be in a Jewish environment, with no whips or guns visible, and to listen to the strains of "*Eli-Eli,*" "*Kol Nidre,*" "*Hatikvah*"—who would not be moved to the depths of one's soul and fail to be spellbound for a little while in spiritual rapture, in a kind of mute, tearful reverie? Only when the final rhapsodic chords of the orchestra faded into silence and I went out into the street, where I again found the forlorn mass, orphaned and starving and tormented—only then did I start running away from that concert. The few minutes of artificially forgetting myself, with no ghettos and forts and massacres, could not withstand the mute, moral disapproval in the eyes of mothers without their children, of orphaned boys and girls. Jewish mourning does not include music, no matter what lofty purposes are ascribed to it.

If the first concerts still had moments of Jewish and artistic exaltation, of forgetting the bitterness of life, of absorbing quiet hopes for better days—a sort of artistic recitation of Psalms for the health of a dear one who is seriously ill—then later they lost this character almost completely. In time the concerts became a commercial venture, with tickets, with patronage, with dressed-up gentlemen and made-up ladies—a place to flirt.

During the most terrible months, when you could touch the danger of ghetto liquidation with your hand, there came the most painful chapter of these concerts. The Nazi rulers who would occasionally attend the public performances of the ghetto orchestra chose that most tragic period to demand special concerts for them alone. At their head was the hangman of the ghetto—Göcke. To these concerts "important people" from Kovno itself would be invited. No Jews, of course, were invited, and if the musicians would have had a choice they would have done without this singular honor. But they were not asked. With broken hearts and artificial smiles on their lips they were forced to entertain their torturers and their hangmen.

This is not the first such fate to befall the Jewish people in its history. The persecutors either wish to sate themselves with Jewish musical talent or they want to lord it over them by forcing them to sing and dance for their tormentors. It all has the same root, however. From "Sing to us the songs of Zion" in Babylonia to the singing and dancing of the Jewish lessee for the landowners in Poland and Lithuania to the Jewish concerts in the Slabodka Ghetto—one thread runs through them: the thread of one long tragedy of the tormented Jewish people. If some of these Jewish musicians remain alive after all this, perhaps a new "by the rivers of Babylon we sat down and wept" may be born, a melody they would not sing for the hangmen but with every stroke of the bow would fill their souls forever with dark memories.

These Jewish concerts for the Gestapo and SS were a thousand times more painful and degrading for the thousands of Jewish mourners than the concerts of Jews for Jews. Perhaps they were a punishment for the musicians and the ghetto leaders who permitted the sound of music to be heard within the mass cemetery of Lithuanian Jewry. Who knows the mysterious ways of the punishing hand?

This matter of the concerts brings to mind a minor incident that left an indelible impression on me.

It was at the first such concert in the ghetto. As though the program had been written especially for the inhabitants of this valley of death, the first number after "*Hatikvah*" was "*Kol Nidre*." The sad, heart-wrenching melody of the Marranos of Spain broke the hearts of the doomed in Slabodka. The mood was tense. All eyes were on the stage, where agonizing tones were being created. A deathly quiet. Suddenly a thud, a scream. A woman had fainted—the woman seated next to me. Until recently she had been a Christian. She could have lived in peace in the city, but she chose to go into the ghetto with her Jewish husband and share the Jewish fate. A latter-day Ruth in Slabodka, a most tragic version.

In the concert hall sat Jews onto whose hearts the "*Kol Nidre*" melody was more deeply engraved. Why was it this Christian woman who was the most deeply moved?

It's hard to know. Perhaps Jews who were rooted in Judaism for a long time had more spiritual strength to endure the suspense of impending death than those who had only recently become Jews. Perhaps that's why the ghettos did not become scenes of mass suicides. There were other Christians in the ghetto for whom the door to the free world out there stood wide open, yet they chose to go with the Jews and perish with them.

The wife of Dr. Matis, a well-known Folkist leader in Lithuania, was a Christian woman and a "pure" German. Her children considered themselves pure Germans. She had three brothers who fought on the war fronts—for Hitler. She could have saved her life, but she was loyal to her Jewish husband and his fate.

Material for a devastating drama is contained in the story of a young Lithuanian convert. He was the son of a Lithuanian diplomat, a consul in the Scandinavian countries. His name was Dr. Juazas Algirdas, and he had fallen in love with a Jewish prostitute. He converted to Judaism and married her. Who knows the ways of the human heart?

When the order was issued driving the Jews into the ghetto, this man went there too along with his wife. The Judenrat gave him a job tending the Jewish gardens that were located right next to the barbed wire. A Lithuanian policeman stationed on the other side of the wire spoke with him a long time one evening and then shot him. He fell with a Christian prayer "Oh Jesus!" on his lips, but his last words were that he wanted to be buried in the Jewish cemetery and that the people in the ghetto should help his wife.

The most moving story, however, is that of a Christian woman (not a convert) who was known to every Jew in the ghetto. We learned about her too from our visitor. Every day one could see an old woman in the ghetto walking around with a young child. The woman looked typically Lithuanian. The kerchief she wore did not do very much to disguise that fact. The language that she and the child spoke was also a source of wonderment. Lithuanian in the ghetto? Those who saw her more than once, however, soon knew the whole story.

The woman was a pious Christian, a Lithuanian. Her child was Jewish on both sides. She had been the housekeeper for the parents of the child for over thirty years. When the child's parents were killed during the first days of the Nazi terror she refused to desert the child. She would go into the city and do the hardest labor so long as she could bring back some food for the child. Each time she did this she risked her own life, crawling through the barbed wire or putting on a yellow star and smuggling herself into Jewish labor brigades. She herself lived on stale bread, but to the Jewish child—who was not even her own—she gave the best she could find.

"Converts are as prickly for Jews as thorns," goes the old saying. Inside the ghetto this was proven false. In the ghetto we knew not only of Lithuanians who were murderers but also of Lithuanians who were Righteous Gentiles. Yes, there were some of those. But some converts couldn't change their spots. One woman convert almost brought about a massacre on Ramygalos Street with her lies and schemes. Even when they were locked up together, many of these converts remained the Jews' worst enemies!

CHAPTER 7

Liberated Mourners

JULY 28

The echoes of the artillery bombardments are becoming clearer and clearer—a sure sign that the front is moving steadily closer to us. The war in the air has also intensified. Every explosion echoes inside each one of us, but we only smile and say: "Well, what did you think of that one?" or "That was a good one!" Every crash adds new hope; every detonation fortifies your faith. The tension is unimaginable. How long have we waited for this moment? Yet how shall we be able to endure these final days? Or maybe these are the final hours? This is the most critical time of all, and who knows? Perhaps the front will stop moving before it reaches us. If the Germans try to dig in here, there could be relentless battles. If that happens, we are lost. Life and death, liberation and defeat, light and shadow—they all run together. Which will win out?

Moyshe, who was hiding nearby with a peasant, Shuki, comes to visit us. He tells us a story that is a mixture of hope and fear, joy and despair. One day he stumbled onto five strangers who had unexpectedly come to visit his protector. Three of them wore Ukrainian uniforms and were armed. Of the other two, one was a young woman also wearing the uniform of a Ukrainian. Had they deserted to the Germans? Moyshe's first thought was that he would not survive to see his dream of living to at least sixty years old. There was no means of retreat. He prepared himself for the worst. But in talking with them he learned that they had run away from a camp somewhere near Kovno and were now waiting for the arrival of the Red Army. They informed him that they were "mobilizing" him to fight against the Germans.

"How come you don't have a weapon? Stalin said that as soon as you escape from a camp you must get yourself a weapon. Come with us and we will get you one."

Small comfort in the last minutes before liberation. He told them about the pain and suffering that Jews had undergone. It made no difference to them at all. Earlier when they were talking with his host, they had come out with the familiar slanders against Jews, which his host had reported to him. Luckily, these characters had had too much to drink so he was able to get away from them and find us.

Our hearts start beating faster. We all agree that no matter who they are, it will be safer for us if they don't show up anywhere near us. In any case, if knowledge of their presence were to reach the ears of the peasants around here, it might also reach the Germans stationed not too far away, and they might begin scouring the bushes, which could mean the end of us too. If, however, the escaped Ukrainians were actually German spies in disguise, that would be an instant tragedy for us. So we are all upset, and we wait fearfully for the next day, for Moyshe to come to see us again and give us further details.

JULY 29

If he had bad news for us, he was supposed to arrive early in the morning. If he didn't show up, that would be a sign that the danger had passed.

Five o'clock. Six. Seven. Ten o'clock, and he had still not arrived. We grow a little calmer. We start comforting each other—maybe we've gotten out of this with merely a sleepless night and an unnecessary packing up of our things. The fear in our faces fades a little. A smile returns. Another trial we have to undergo on the eve of our liberation.

Suddenly we all jump up and look to the west. We can hear it clearly—seven rifle shots, one after the other. The sounds are coming from the direction of Moyshe's hiding place. Are the shots coming from the rifles of their five visitors? The question is frozen in our eyes. No one dares utter a word, but each of us knows what the other is thinking. Suddenly, into the bushes our Barbora comes running toward us looking like a ghost.

"Quick! Get away from here! Run!"

She responds to our frightened looks in disconnected phrases: "Two tanks—during the night—at my neighbor Shuki—killed the entire family in the house—burned it down—an informer."

This only strengthens our suspicion that the five Ukrainians were spies for the Germans. First they questioned all the peasants suspected by the Germans; then the German soldiers came to finish the spies' dirty work through extermination. We hold a brief conference and decide to get away from here at once, even though it is still daylight. The danger is so close that we should not stay here another hour. Flight is the only answer.

So we start out again across fields and through woods, stopping every so often to listen for unwanted footsteps. Finally, after a long search for proper cover, we find the right bushes, not too far from Barbora and Tadeusz. My wife starts feeling faint and we barely revive her with the one bottle of water that we fortunately had.

The rest of that day we have no food or water. Darkness falls. We hear no unusual sounds coming from the direction of the old couple's house. The dog does not bark. No one cries out. No revolver shots. We confer again. We must move closer to the house and find out what is going on in the neighborhood. We can't just stay here like sitting ducks, waiting. It's quite possible that it is too dangerous to stay anywhere near the place now.

We move closer to the house and, when the darkness is at its densest, Nechama slips over to the door. It's locked. The horse and pig are gone too, which means that the old couple have gone away. A bad sign. We could be walking into a trap. We cannot stay here another minute. And we can't ask any questions of the neighbors. What to do?

Seemingly out of nowhere, Tadeusz suddenly appears. He is angry with us for coming so close to the house. Any moment those same characters could be back. We put our bundles on our backs and start moving.

JULY 30

A night of anguish, of terrible pictures in our heads. The old man has disappeared. We have had no news. We lie inert, as in a sack. Moreover, we are beginning to suffer hunger pangs. No less painful is the feeling that we are sitting on a volcano. Around midday a tremendous bombardment starts. It seems as if the guns are right next to us. The shocks are terrifying—but they make us happy. The unspoken question in our eyes is—"Maybe?"

The old man was supposed to have visited us this morning. Where is he? What has happened to him? The front lines are certainly close enough, and yet we don't know where we are and whether we should even be here. The latest news is a life-and-death matter for us. But how are we to get it? We cover ourselves with fallen branches and lie down to wait for old Tadeusz, who is now our only salvation.

It is later that same evening. The setting sun is sending its last rays to the tips of the highest trees when he finally reappears. His expression seems less clouded than yesterday. His eyes are more alert and more cheerful. With bated breath we wait for the answer to our question: "What is happening?"

He smiles in his easygoing, peasant fashion: "Good news. You can stop worrying."

Then he calmly lights his pipe and gives us the details: "The Red Army has already taken Kovno. It's not too far from our place. You'll be free soon. Come back with me so you'll be closer to the house."

This is completely unexpected. Sudden happiness, like sudden fear, often numbs the heart and the brain. But we can't build any castles in the air on the word of the old man. In our situation a moment's tardiness can cost you your life. Just today we had seen German soldiers, and in these parts, among isolated woods and bushes, that is a rare sight. They were looking for horses. But since the peasants had been hiding their horses in the bushes, the Germans had taken to searching the thickets, where instead of a horse they might sometimes find a Jew.

The honor of receiving such German soldiers had fallen to a peasant in the vicinity. In response to his complaint that some other Germans had already taken his horses, the reply was that many partisans were hiding in these woods, and if the peasant refused to reveal the partisans' whereabouts, he and his family would come to an unfortunate end. The Germans had then set up machine guns all around his house. Luckily the peasant kept a cool head and the matter went no further than a warning. All this had happened less than two hundred yards away from us! If we ever get out of this alive, we will probably wonder how we managed to endure such a hail of close calls, such a long series of emotional shocks, without our hearts bursting into pieces.

AUGUST 2

In the last few days, the sounds of battle have grown louder and louder. The shells are actually flying over our heads. We can hear their awful whistling. We can hear explosions close by. Apparently, we are between the German and Soviet firing positions. It would be dangerous for us to leave this spot now, so we stay put. For hours we lie here with our faces to the ground, buried among the shrubs with artillery fire whizzing over us. Raise your head for a moment—whoosh!—and then you have to hit the dirt right away. Our nerves are strained to the breaking point.

"So this is how it's going to end for us?" I venture. "All that we've gone through—and in the last minute to be killed by a blind bullet?"

How can you describe the feelings of a person who is standing on the threshold of a liberation that they may not live to see?

From participants in the First World War we used to hear stories about miracles. One man was hit by a bullet that glanced off the hard peak of his cap. Another was hit by a grenade that ripped his trousers apart but left his legs unharmed. A third found himself in a trench where his comrade was killed by a bomb, but he himself was untouched. When you go through an experience like this yourself you are not so quick to dismiss such stories as exaggerations. The old woman, for example, tells us when she brings us our soup that under the tree where we had been hiding the day before there had been a burst of shrapnel fire. Out of her pocket she takes a piece of metal to prove it. That entire area under the tree, she says, is as full of holes as a sieve.

Furthermore, today a column of forty German soldiers marched through the very spot in the woods where we were hiding the day before yesterday. Was it luck, intuition, or prophecy to get away from those places a couple of hours before they became fatal? Or was it really a miracle? Several days earlier, before they burned down the house of the neighbor Shuki—along with everyone in it—we had planned to move in there, but we changed our minds. A miracle?

A friend of ours, along with a few other Jews, was in a place where some German police were chasing a Lithuanian. They caught him and shot him, just eight yards from where they lay stretched out in the low grass, expecting the worst. The Germans just didn't take the few extra steps in their direction. A miracle?

On February 24, when eight Gestapo men and some Lithuanian police attacked Antanas's house, there were two Jews there who had brought us the letter from the ghetto. At that particular moment they were inside the house and not, as usual, in the barn. There was no time to run out, so one of them squeezed into the chicken coop below the big oven. The second crawled under a bed. When the Gestapo men went to search the barn, both Jews quickly climbed up into the attic. Before the Gestapo left, they came back and searched the house again. This time in the coop and under the bed. Is there another word for this other than *miracle*?

AUGUST 3

The gunfire from the battles has ceased, and the night in the bushes passes uneventfully. Half the night we sit up, wide awake. The last few hours we doze. With the dawn, the old woman Barbora comes running to us, yelling, something she rarely did. "You're free! The Red Army—already at my neighbor's—come out of the bushes—come into the house—" She is so excited she can hardly get the words out. Her face is lit up with happiness and rejoicing.

We, the few Jews who had managed to flee from the valley of death, stare at her and at one another. A peculiar emotion overwhelms us. We look at old Barbora and she looks at us. All of us are somehow disconcerted. Something is making us uncomfortable.

During the dark days, as we lay hidden, we imagined that at the moment of liberation we would start dancing for joy, we would kiss each other again and again, we would weep, we would sing. There would be no limit to how we would celebrate. But now, when the dream has turned to reality, we are standing there so coldly, so frozen, so . . . lost. What is happening to us?

Up until this moment, it seems, we were carried along by sheer momentum. The shadow of death had pursued us, and we kept running away from it with every bit of our strength. We never looked back, although running blindly like that we had lost mother and father, brothers and sisters, friends. In the fear of death and in the delusion of death we had leapt across their dead bodies. Now that the Angel of Death has disappeared, with it has gone the momentum that had carried us on its wings for weeks, months, years. Now we suddenly see them all clearly: parents, dead; brothers, dead; sisters, dead; friends, dead. All at once there rises before our eyes the horrible image of three and a half years of Hitler's ghetto, three years of slaughter, and in all its horror the question hangs in the air: "Where are they all now? Where?"

Not until this moment do we wake up. Suddenly. As from a horrible dream. And we begin to feel like orphans. Not until this moment did we see each other as deserted and forgotten. A world full of gravestones opens up before us, not a world full of happiness and freedom. The sun is shining again, yes, but how many of us will enjoy it? A new life is arising, yes, but for what minuscule portion of us? A person who has felt the hangman's noose around his neck and been reprieved at the last moment, such a person dances with gratitude. But how many of our dear ones will join us in our happiness? A person who has worn a hangman's noose and been freed at the last moment jumps with joy because his life will now go on and because soon he will go home and put his arms around his mother and father, around his sisters and brothers, and cry out: "I was saved! I was saved!"

But our homes are destroyed; our parents, sisters, and brothers have been murdered and lie in mass graves. To whom should we run with the good news: "We are saved!"? There are many more dead than there are alive, and their silenced voices, crying out in the void "We are here," are far stronger than ours. So the heart breaks and the cry "We are saved!" remains frozen on our lips.

These conflicting emotions of grief and joy, of hope and despair, of rescue and bereavement, are the reasons we cannot even move to embrace our liberators; it is the reason we remain frozen on the spot, and only a sorrowful smile hangs at the corners of our lips. What is left of us? Cold skulls, dry bones, living shadows. Will it ever be otherwise? Will we someday be able—like other human beings, even like animals—to rejoice in the rising sun, in the blossoming springtime, in the singing of the birds?

We are filled with grief!

AUGUST 4

We drive these mournful thoughts away and try to crawl out of our ten-month-old burrow. The fear of the people who have dominated us does not vanish immediately. We still walk unsteadily. We still speak in whispers. We still hesitate to utter a Yiddish word aloud. And if anyone does raise his voice, we still warn him, "*Sh-sh!* Not so loud!"

We have not yet seen any Red Army soldiers, and we still don't believe that this is really us walking on the grass in the middle of the day without any thought of fleeing into the bushes.

Unobstructed views open up before our eyes. This is not a rhetorical statement. It is a deeply felt emotion. These expressions are empty concepts to a free individual who always had a limitless sky before his eyes. For such a person, the words are nothing but flowery language. We, however, who for months that seemed as long as years saw only little slivers of sky through the openings in the bushes or through a crack in the barn door—for us, how wonderful it is to see the free horizons again.

The fear of other human beings gradually disappears. Our step grows firmer. The dreamlike veil grows flimsier and the reality becomes more and more visible: We are free! It is true! We hurry in the direction where we think the Red Army is.

On the way we meet the shepherd Antoniuk. He was our nightmare during the entire ten months. A clever, cunning lad who stuck his nose into everything and who had such an uncanny sense of where Jews were hiding that we were especially careful to avoid him. In addition, he had a glib tongue, and whatever he noticed he immediately broadcast throughout the whole village.

Now he stood before us, this twelve-year-old big shot, looking like a whipped child, without his former luster, and we said to ourselves: This is the object we were so afraid of? And he stands there smiling to himself: Aha, so they were here, these *Zhids*. I knew it all the time! But now we don't even give another thought about him. We continue on our way to find our liberators.

AUGUST 7

We spend a few more days here helping the old couple with their chores—taking in the hay, gathering the corn, reinforcing the supports of the barn.

But how much longer can we stand it? We want to see other Jews. Although we know that most of our friends and acquaintances are no longer alive, we don't give up hope. So we start packing for the journey. "Packing" for us is just a word. There is nothing to pack. The little bit of food and clothing that we do have takes only a couple of minutes to pack. But saying goodbye is not that easy. That we would ever find it difficult to leave this place never occurred to us. We dreamed about the happy moments when we would be rescued and could start for home—but never in our wildest dreams did we think we would feel so connected to this place where we were saved. Who understands the mysterious ways of the human soul?

Ten months! The deadly dangers and the feelings of gratitude created invisible threads of love between us and the old couple. Only during the minutes when we became certain we would live did we begin to feel our attachment to this place, where extraordinary people had saved us from death. Even the broken-down old cottage and the crumbling barn became dear to us, as did the thick bushes, the loyal dog, the horse, and more than anything else the two old Lithuanians. We used to call them *Tevialis* and *Mamita* (Little Father and Little Mother), but only now do we become aware that these were not idle words but a reflection of feelings whose genuineness we did not understand until the moment of separation.

The heart aches. The tears brim over. Obviously, these moments of parting are just as difficult for the old couple too. They had grown accustomed to the hustle and bustle. Henceforth they will be alone again, alone in the woods, on their piece of barren land. But we could not stay here.

We say farewell to old Tadeusz. No one's eyes are dry. The old man comforts us: "Don't worry. We'll see each other again. Don't cry. Be happy that you're free again. We'll come to visit you in the city. Be happy!"

We walk out of that cottage as if we were leaving a funeral—that's how connected we felt to the old couple.

The old woman accompanies us for a while as we walk to the highway. Mostly we are silent, our hearts heavy. We are troubled by the thought that she and Tadeusz are not only remaining all alone but that they will continue to lead their lives of bitter poverty. (In fact we did see Tadeusz again quite soon. A month or so later we summoned him to come with his wagon to the city. We loaded it up with furniture and other items from abandoned houses of Jews. This was like a fortune to him.)

We are at the highway. We stop. Our hearts are pounding. The moment of parting is upon us. Embraces. Kisses. Tears. Again and again. We don't seem to be able to leave, to separate. But it is inevitable. Now we are walking in opposite directions. I turn around. I see the old woman's back, the white kerchief on her head. With slow steps she is moving farther and farther away from us. We are going in one direction, she in another. The tragic fate of humanity lies deep in this simple act of separation.

We walk part of the way and ride part of it on Red Army trucks. Finally we are in Kovno, walking through the ghetto. Utter desolation. On this relatively large area where some 30,000 Jews had lived there are now only chimneys—lonely black chimneys, a reminder of the lives and the homes that were destroyed. Everything has been burned to the ground. What the peasants have been telling us—and what we refused to believe—we now see with our own eyes. Here is a mound of corpses; some had been burned to death, some had suffocated, in a cellar that was blown up. Over there is a hand, half chewed up by a dog. Bodies are scattered all over—entire families, lone individuals, tiny Jewish babies. I pick up one of the dead children. My hands are trembling, my knees are buckling, the ground under my feet is quaking . . .

And the dead child is pleading, weeping, screaming . . .

"Hush, my little angel, hush—now you can sleep in peace . . ."

AUGUST 8

The long, exhausting forty kilometers from Karalgiris to Kovno, the unnerving scenes of destruction in the ghetto, even the first night in a decent bed, without a dog for a watchman—all this does not allow us to keep our eyes closed for very long. After a few hours sleep is out of the question. Impatiently and under great stress, we somehow get through the night. In the early morning hours we are already out on the street. First we must keep a deathbed promise. A neighbor of ours from Kovno had made us swear that if we survived we would find her ten-year-old daughter, Baylinka, who had been hiding in the home of a Lithuanian woman on Green Hill, a suburb of Kovno. We go directly to the place—a small house squeezed in between two large buildings.

Children are playing in the yard. We ask them a few questions to make sure we are in the right place. Suddenly there is a scream. Crying, running, a little girl has broken away from the other children and is running home. She turns her head to see if anyone is pursuing her, and only then do we notice—below her peasant kerchief—the face of a Jewish child.

"Baylinka! Baylinka!" We follow her. Opening the door we hear her childish cries: "*Zhidey . . . Zhidey . . .*" ("Jews . . . Jews . . .") Baylinka is standing with both her arms around the waist of an impoverished middle-aged woman; her face is buried in the woman's apron, but her two dark Jewish eyes are staring at us in fear.

"Baylinka, don't you recognize us?"

No reply.

"Baylinka, don't you remember that we used to live in the same house on Ratusze Place?"

Silence.

"Baylinka, don't you understand Yiddish?"

She presses closer against the peasant apron and shakes her head from side to side. The woman explains to us that Baylinka cannot simply disregard what she had been taught to say during the two years that she was hidden. She still cannot grasp the fact that she is free, that she no longer needs to be afraid of anyone.

Little by little Baylinka becomes accustomed to us again, although she still answers our questions in Lithuanian. When we sit down at the table we notice a shiny little crucifix around her neck. It's something that doesn't belong with her Jewish face.

From underneath a bed she removes a little box. Her uncle had once given it to her, she tells us. She takes out two photographs. In one she is standing with her two-year-old sister, who had been hidden at the other end of Lithuania. The second photograph is of her mother. "Uncle Reuben told me never to lose this picture. That's my mother . . ." Who is strong enough not to weep?

This is our first meeting with a liberated Jew, a little Jewish girl with a crucifix around her neck. What about all the other Jewish children who weren't wearing one? Why were they murdered? Are there exceptions to the holy commandment "Thou shalt not kill"?

After leaving Baylinka, we go out to look for other survivors.

It is now two weeks after liberation. In the yard of a house where the survivors are gathering, groups of Jews stand around talking. The only subject is—names. Did you see that one? Did you ever meet this one? Every newcomer is immediately surrounded and bombarded with those questions. It may be someone whom you may have seen only once before in your life, yet you embrace him like a long-lost brother. Or you may not even know him, but you embrace him and kiss him and you both sob anyway—out of happiness merely to be another survivor, and out of sorrow because others are not there and will never be there for this reunion.

The longer we stay at this gathering place the sadder we grow. This is all that is left of Jewish Kovno? Not even one other member of your family? Not even one of your friends? Some Jews were evacuated; some were burned alive in the ghetto itself. Your own rescue shrinks to insignificance in the face of the deaths of so many others.

You shake hands again. *Sholem aleykhem.* You kiss each other again. But an invisible hand seems to interpose itself in each embrace. Such is the happiness of Jews rescued from Hitler's inferno.

There is no joy in being reborn.

No delight in going forth to start a new life.

We are standing upon graves, graves that are still fresh. And death has its arms wrapped around all of us. Long, skeletal fingers press us all together.

We, the survivors, carry so many deaths along with us. Who knows who will conquer whom?

Dead lives prepare to build new lives. Will they succeed? Can they succeed?

LAST WORD

I am reading the pages of my diary twelve years after they were written. I can hardly believe they are pages of "my" life.

Could a human being endure all that? Did people really go through all that? Yes. All of it!

Inhuman suffering calls forth inhuman strength. May this story always remain as a reminder—and as an inspiration.

Front cover (left) and interior pages (below) from one of the two notebooks in which Berl Kagan kept the diary of his ten-month experience in hiding during World War II. These diaries are preserved in the archives of the YIVO Institute for Jewish Research in New York City.

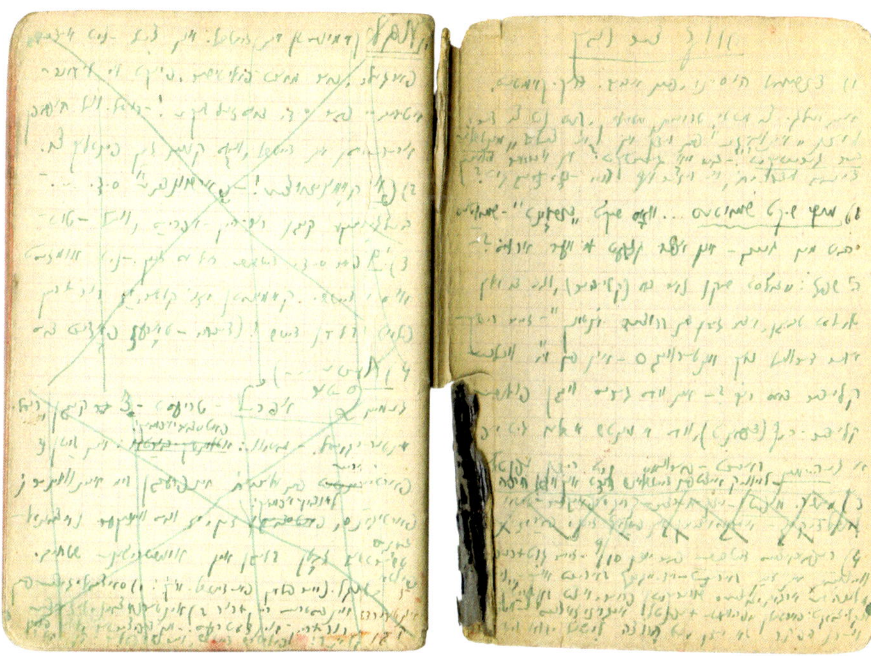

Berl and Raja Ilman Kagan in Lithuania before the war

Berl Kagan (front row, wearing glasses and holding a flag) with members of the Zionist youth group Hapoel, 1935

From *Hidden History of the Kovno Ghetto*, United States Holocaust Memorial Museum

Nechama Ilman

Barbora Urbonaviciute-Baceviciene (wife of Tadeusz Pocius) (far left) circa late 1960s

Embroidered tapestry by Raja Kagan used to wrap photos and documents, which she hid near her home in Kovno. Long after the war ended Raja framed the tapestry and gave it to her granddaughter Judy Camassar.

Bag used by Raja Kagan to hide the embroidered tapestry holding photos and documents

Stanislava (Stasia) Volskiene, wife of Antanas Volskis

Tadeusz Pocius (sitting), who helped hide the Kagan family, with Antanas Volskis, a Lithuanian who helped arrange for their escape from the ghetto and assisted them during their time in hiding

Concerts performed in the Kovno Ghetto were the subject of controversy among performers and audience members.

United States Holocaust Memorial Museum, courtesy of Robert W. Hofmekler & Yad Vashem Photo Archive, Jerusalem

The probable route taken by Tadeusz Pocius when transporting Berl, Raja, and Nechama from the Kovno Ghetto to his home in Karalgiris (provided by Tadeusz's and Barbora's granddaughter and great-granddaughter)

KAUNAS GHETTO

- 1 – Gates
- 2 – The Ghetto Jewish Council
- 3 – Small hospital
- 4 – Slabodka Yeshiva
- 5 – Large hospital
- T – Bridge between the small and large ghettos
- Cemetery
- Barbed wire fence
- Reduction of the ghetto August 15, 1941
- Reduction of the small ghetto October 4, 1941
- Reduction of the ghetto January 11, 1942
- Reduction of the ghetto October 1943
- Reduction of the ghetto December 22, 1943

Berl and Raja with their children, Heskel and Miriam, and Raja's sister Nechama in Rome after the war

Berl Kagan on the balcony of the YIVO Institute for Jewish Research in New York City (while it was still located on Fifth Ave., across from Central Park)

Berl Kagan with his sister-in-law, Nechama Ilman Himmel, visiting New York City from Israel around 1980

Afterword

BY MIRIAM KAGAN LIEBER

It was only by chance that I realized the original notebooks used by my father, Berl Kagan, for his diary were housed in the archives of the YIVO Institute for Jewish Research in New York. After his death in 1993, I had donated all his papers to the YIVO, never imagining I would need to revisit them. Nearly three decades passed before I looked again.

In 2022, during my efforts to publish the English translation of his Yiddish diary, *A yid in vald*, several historians in Lithuania suggested that valuable documentation might lie dormant within that donation. At their urging I contacted Leo Greenbaum, the YIVO's accessions archivist, to request an inventory of my father's papers. To my amazement, the list included two original notebooks. I had long believed that my father's handwritten diary—kept while hiding in the forests of Lithuania during the Holocaust—had been lost or discarded long ago.

Soon after, I found myself sitting in the YIVO's reference room, holding those two worn and fragile notebooks—documents over seventy-five years old, their yellowed, weathered pages blotchy and brittle from time and exposure. I was overwhelmed. These were the very notebooks that had accompanied my father throughout his nine months in a Lithuanian forest, through his journey to Italy, where he stayed for five years after the war, and finally to the United States.

I could not help but wonder: How did he manage to write in the forest? How did he find paper and ink? Did he begin with one notebook and later somehow acquire another, or had he carried both with him from the start? How did he protect them—these delicate volumes—as he and his small group were forced to flee again and again, running for their lives with only what they could carry? Whether standing in the rain, hiding in a hut, or trudging through the mud in the dark of night, were the notebooks always with him?

I will never know the answers to these questions. But I do know this: Even in the face of almost certain death, my father believed that documenting what he saw and endured was essential. He believed that truth, once written, could outlive him. He believed, as he did for the rest of his life, that history must not be forgotten.

Berl Kagan is no longer with us, but his diary lives on. These words, once scrawled under impossible conditions, have now crossed languages and time to reach a new generation of readers.

I am the middle of three children. My brother Heskel and I were both born in Rome, Italy, where my parents and my aunt fled shortly after emerging from hiding. They had learned that the Nazis had been driven from Lithuania by the Red Army, but my father's name was on a list of those to be deported to Siberia. How they managed to travel all the way to Italy, I do not know.

In 1950 our family came to the United States, sponsored by my great-aunt Chana Berman. My sister Ada was born soon after in Philadelphia. My father, being a journalist and writer, sought work in New York, and we moved to Brooklyn. My mother's sister, Nechama Ilman, chose to go to Palestine, where she married another refugee.

Like so many refugees and survivors, my parents spoke little of the past. They wanted a new life for us, free from shadows. And yet, *A Jew in the Woods* has helped me understand so much more about who they were, and about the traces the past left on all of us.

For instance, my mother insisted we never leave food on our plates. We rarely ate out and never traveled. I was raised with a deep awareness of cost—of food, of clothes, of anything that might seem dispensable. She rarely bought anything for herself, but she was quick to help a neighbor who needed a coat or food. Even at home, she carried a quiet preparedness: She told me to always lay out my clothes and important documents before going to sleep, in case we had to flee in the night—a habit I still follow. She was deeply private and warned us never to share personal information with others.

My father, on the other hand, never stopped believing in the importance of historical memory. Almost every weekend he and I would take the train from Brooklyn to the New York Public Library—he to do research, I to spend hours in the children's section. He was always writing air-mail letters to people around the world, though many were to Lithuania. When I asked who he was writing to, he would simply say "an old woman." Only later did I come to believe it was Barbora, the Lithuanian woman who, with her husband Tadeusz, helped save their lives.

Though they didn't speak much about the war, fragments still surfaced. My mother once told me she had helped deliver a baby in the Kovno Ghetto. When they escaped, she buried a bag of photos and documents near their house and they were still there after the war. I have them to this day.

She once told me that she dreamt my father should not report for what the Nazis called an "action." He listened to her—and everyone who did report was killed. She believed in the meaning of dreams.

My aunt Nechama, who looked and sounded like any other Lithuanian, was able to sneak potatoes into the ghetto while returning from forced labor at a German airfield. When my father first raised the idea of escape, my mother initially refused—she did not want to leave his ill mother behind. Only after my grandmother died and my mother sewed her burial shroud by hand did she agree to flee.

Some marks never left them. My mother once told me she no longer had to shave her legs. The hair had stopped growing during their time in the forest. The skin had frozen.

Now, decades later, I understand more fully the silences and habits that shaped our home. This diary—my father's voice, his memories, his truth—offers a window into the unimaginable and a lasting record of survival, courage, and the enduring need to remember.

As my father wrote at the end of *A yid in vald*: "May this story always remain as a reminder—and as an inspiration."

This publication marks the culmination of a journey that began in an unexpected way.

My cousin Marc Katz and his partner, Andrew Quinn, were traveling through Lithuania on vacation. They happened to mention their cousin, Berl Kagan (Kahn), to a local tour guide. To their surprise, the name was familiar. The guide referred them to the Vilna Gaon Museum of Jewish History in Vilnius, where they met Danutė Selčinskaja and Stanislovas Stasiulis. That encounter became the catalyst that set everything in motion.

Soon after, I was introduced to Danutė and Stanislovas via Zoom. What began as an initial meeting soon grew into an ongoing dialogue. When they learned of the existence of an English-language draft of the wartime diary, new doors opened—both for me and for the museum.

Conversations with Danutė, Stanislovas, Marc, and my cousins Zaro Weil and Gareth Jenkins deepened my understanding of the diary's importance and its potential impact. It became clear that this document, written by my father, needed to be made accessible to a wider audience.

During the war, my father deliberately omitted last names from the diary to protect those involved, fearing that if the manuscript were discovered, it could cost people their lives. Astonishingly, Danutė was able to recover those missing names. Through her work at the museum—researching Lithuanians who hid Jews during the Holocaust—she had independently documented the three couples mentioned in the diary who had risked their lives to protect eight Jews. However, she lacked a first-hand account to corroborate that research. *A yid in vald* provided the vital testimony that confirmed her findings.

This confirmation led to a powerful act of recognition. Yad Vashem, The World Holocaust Remembrance Center in Israel, honored Tadeusz and Barbora Pocius as Righteous Among the Nations. In Lithuania, they were posthumously awarded the Life Savior Cross, which was accepted by their granddaughters in a moving ceremony that affirmed their bravery and sacrifice.

This book is not only a testimony of survival and courage—it is a bridge between past and present, memory and history. It is my hope that by sharing this story, the legacy of those who risked everything to do what was right will live on.

Acknowledgments

Bringing this book to completion has been a deeply rewarding intellectual and emotional journey, and I am profoundly grateful to those who supported me along the way.

A heartfelt thank you to my cousin Marc Katz for his unwavering belief in the importance of preparing my father's diary for publication in English. His vision, encouragement, and research set things in motion.

To my cousins, Zaro (Phyllis) Weil and Gareth Jenkins—your guidance, insight, and the countless hours you devoted to this project meant more than words can convey. Phyllis, your creativity and generous spirit supported and uplifted me in more ways than I can express. Gareth, your sharp eye, thoughtful feedback, and deep knowledge of publishing were invaluable. Phyllis and Gareth, your presence—both intellectually and emotionally—was a constant source of strength and played a vital role in bringing this work to life.

To Danutė Selčinskaja, Drew Quinn, and Leo Greenbaum—thank you all for your support.

To Stanislavos Stasiulis, a gifted historian in Lithuania who generously shared his knowledge and helped clarify important details—thank you. I am now honored to consider you a friend.

Thank you to Rebecca Frankel, Sam Kassow, and Justin Cammy for their generous and valued endorsements of this translation.

Special thanks to the team at the Yiddish Book Center, whose professionalism and guidance helped bring this project into its final form.

To everyone who showed support in ways big and small: Whether you shared an encouraging word, asked how the writing was going, or just believed in me from the sidelines, thank you.

Finally, I am grateful beyond measure to my family—my husband, Marty Lieber; my children, Judy Camassar (and her husband Todd) and Ken Lieber (and his wife Debbie); and my grandchildren, Ross and Brooke Camassar, and Mikayla and Brandon Lieber. Your steadfast support, understanding, and encouragement through all the ups and downs of publishing kept me focused and determined. Much love always.

My father, Berl Kagan (Kahn) is no longer alive to see this English edition of his diary, but his words remain vivid, powerful, and deeply human. His belief in the value of documenting history was unwavering. This book is a memorial to his determination and vision.

Miriam Kagan Lieber

Biographies

BERL KAGAN (1908-1993)

Berl Kagan (Kahn) was a Jewish writer, lexicographer, bibliographer, editor, and Holocaust survivor whose postwar scholarship contributed significantly to the preservation and reconstruction of Eastern European Jewish history and Yiddish literature.

He was born in Telz (Telšiai), Lithuania, and received a traditional Jewish education in religious schools and the preparatory program for the renowned Telz Yeshiva. In 1930, he completed his studies at the Hebrew Teachers' Seminary in Kovno (Kaunas), after which he taught religion in the Tarbut Hebrew school system.

Kagan was deeply involved in Jewish socialist and Zionist politics. He served as general secretary of the Zionist Socialist Party and of the League for Working Israel in Lithuania. His political engagement extended to the international sphere, where he was a delegate to the Zionist Congresses in Lucerne (1935) and Geneva (1939). Parallel to his political activities, he contributed regularly to *Di tsayt* (*The Time*), the Yiddish organ of the Zionist Socialist Party in Kovno, and from 1935 to 1940 he served as replacement editor of the daily *Dos vort* (*The Word*).

During the German occupation of Lithuania, Kagan was interned in the Kovno Ghetto, where he was active in the underground resistance and served on the Central Committee of the Zionist Socialist Party. In October 1943, he and his wife, Raja Ilman (married in 1939), escaped from the ghetto and were hidden in the village of Karalgiris by two Lithuanian peasants, Tadeusz Pocius and Barbora

Urbonavičiūtė-Bacevičienė, until August 1944, when Lithuania was liberated from the Germans. Antanas Volskis arranged the rescue. Also involved during the period of their hiding were Stanislava Volskienė, Leonas Vaidotas, and Stanilava Vaidotienė.

Following the Soviet reoccupation of Lithuania, Kagan was targeted for deportation to Siberia. He fled the country with his wife and sister-in-law, Nechama, eventually arriving in Italy. Between 1945 and 1950 he lived among Jewish displaced persons and played a key role in the cultural and intellectual reconstruction of survivor communities. He was a founding member of the Union of Jewish Writers, Journalists, and Artists in Italy, served on its board from 1946 to 1949, and was elected chairman in 1949. Kagan also served on the Central Committee of the Organization of Jewish Refugees and edited *Baderekh* (*On the Road*), a Yiddish-language journal for displaced Jews, while contributing to *In gang* (*On the Way*), published by the Jewish Writers Association.

In 1950 Kagan immigrated to the United States and settled in New York. Between 1951 and 1954 he taught in Jewish supplementary schools before joining the YIVO Institute for Jewish Research in 1955. He remained at the YIVO until 1967, after which he served as a librarian at the Jewish Theological Seminary until 1980. Notably, Kagan passed away while speaking by phone with Dina Abramowitz, head librarian at the YIVO, discussing what would have been his final major project, *Lexicon of Jewish Writers Part II.*

Kagan's scholarly contributions are of considerable significance to the study of Jewish history and Yiddish literature. His *Lexicon of Yiddish Writers* (1986), received the National Jewish Book Award, and remains one of the most comprehensive reference works on Yiddish literary figures. Another monumental achievement is *Seyfer haprenumerantn* (*Hebrew Subscription Lists*), a bibliographic index documenting over 8,700 Jewish communities throughout Europe and North Africa, drawn from historical rabbinic and literary subscription lists. This work, the result of over 15 years of research, remains a unique and indispensable tool for scholars investigating Jewish communal and intellectual networks.

Among his other notable works is *Jewish Cities, Towns and Vil-*

lages in Lithuania until 1918: Historical-Biographical Sketches, which preserves the memory and character of Lithuanian Jewish communities prior to their destruction. Kagan also served as editor for multiple *Yizkor* (memorial) books, including those dedicated to the communities of Suvalk, Szydłowiec, Luboml, and Zwoleń. He was a contributor and editor for volume 8 of the *Biographical Dictionary of Modern Yiddish Literature*.

Berl Kagan (Kahn)'s life and scholarship reflect a profound commitment to cultural preservation in the face of rupture and loss. His editorial and bibliographic work constitutes a major contribution to Jewish historiography, particularly in the fields of Holocaust studies, East European Jewish history, and Yiddish literature. As both a witness and a chronicler, Kagan ensured that the voices of lost communities and marginalized writers would continue to resonate in scholarly discourse and collective memory.

MAX ROSENFELD (1913–1997)

A Yiddish translator and editor of over twenty-five books, Max Rosenfeld was faculty at both Gratz College and the International Institute for Secular Humanistic Judaism, director of the Jewish Children's Folkshul in Philadelphia from 1963 to 1975, and a monthly columnist on "Our Secular Jewish Heritage" in *Jewish Currents* magazine for thirty years.

About White Goat Press

White Goat Press, the Yiddish Book Center's imprint, is committed to bringing newly translated work to the widest readership possible in English. We publish work in all genres—novels, short stories, drama, poetry, memoirs, essays, reportage, plays, and popular fiction, including romance and detective stories.

WHITE GOAT PRESS

whitegoatpress.org

The Yiddish Book Center's imprint